HOME MADE simple

FOR KIDS

HOME MADE simple

FOR KIDS

STYLISH, CRAFTY PROJECTS
TO MAKE WITH AND FOR YOUR KIDS

Joanna Gosling

Photography by Rachel Whiting

Kyle Books

For Maya, Jona and Honor

First published in Great Britain in 2014 by
Kyle Books, an imprint of Kyle Cathie Ltd
192–198 Vauxhall Bridge Road
London, SW1V 1DX
general.enquiries@kylebooks.com
www.kylebooks.com

Printer line 10 9 8 7 6 5 4 3 2 1

ISBN 978 0 85783 104 0

Editors: Catharine Robertson and Tara O'Sullivan
Copy Editor: Salima Hirani
Designer: Christine Sullivan
Photographer: Rachel Whiting
Props Stylist: Lucy Bloomfield
Production: Lisa Pinnell

Please enjoy these projects and make as many as you want for yourself or as gifts for friends and family. The designs are not to be used for commercial use.

A Cataloguing in Publication record for this title is available from the British Library.

Colour reproduction by ALTA London
Printed and bound in China by 1010 Printing International Ltd.

CONTENTS

INTRODUCTION

As a mother of three children, a large proportion of the things I make is for their space, for their stuff and for them.

I create my makes by thinking of what will work most effectively in a particular space, or for a particular use, and I translate it into the simplest way to make it. My daughters' bedrooms are almost entirely handmade because I just kept coming up against practical issues I wanted to fix in order to make life a bit simpler. For instance, needing a place in which to stash books, a drink and anything else they wanted while sleeping in bunks led to the creation of wall-mounted wooden wine boxes by each bunk. Wanting a quick and easy way to make their beds in the morning (especially the top bunk!) resulted in turning their duvets into smart but simple quilts. Frustrated with a constantly messy wardrobe that didn't have enough useful space, I replaced it with fruit crates along one wall, covered with a makeshift curtain.

I love to make simple things for the kids to wear, too. My mother used to make us beautiful handmade outfits, faithfully following proper patterns. I've never tried to master the skill of following sewing patterns, due to lack of time and patience. But I do have a powerful desire to make, and I am always creating simple designs in my head that don't require any pattern, keeping the whole job simple and quick. If you've read my books before, you might know my mantra is 'minimum effort, maximum return'. To this end, making pretty skirts, for instance, takes about 15 minutes. Making baggy trousers requires only a teensy bit more effort. Once you know the basic drill for making these things, you can whizz them up super quick. And you can make nicer and cheaper garments than those you can buy.

Aside from the fact that making something is always time well spent (because you've either solved a problem, or come up with something nice to wear, use or look at), a very important part of the making process is that it gives you something else – time to breathe. People always ask me how I have time to make the things I do. In our busy lives, it's easy to do away with any task that doesn't have to be done. No one *has* to make anything. Most things can be sourced fairly (or very) cheaply – flatpack furniture and throwaway fashion.

But when you take the time to make something, it's as if the world has stopped for a while. Going out shopping, enjoyable as it can be, can become frenetic. It's certainly not relaxing. When you've sat quietly for a while and made something, you don't just get your lovely 'I did that' creation to show for your effort – the quiet time it's given you is a bonus that improves your wellbeing in so many ways. It's good for the mind and soul – simple satisfaction. That's why I make. And that's why I am passionate about passing it on, to adults and to kids.

Any parent knows that children love making things and, left on their own with a few basic crafty bits and bobs, they can surprise you with where their imaginations will lead them.

What I hope to do in the 'by kids' section of this book is to empower children to unleash their imaginations by showing how easy it is to make something fabulous with very basic ingredients. The safety pin bracelet on page 92 is a perfect example of this. Take something functional and everyday and, with a little creativity, you can turn it into something special.

There are no rules on who can make what in this book. But nominally, the 'for kids' section is filled with things adults can make, while the 'by kids' section contains things kids can make themselves, with or without adult involvement. When I say 'kids', I mean a child of any age from five upwards. Some of the projects can be made unaided by children of most ages. Others need more collaboration, depending on the age or ability of the child.

Underpinning everything I make is the importance of keeping it simple. Don't turn making into a palaver. That undermines the joy of it. So don't worry about perfection. I cut corners wherever I can. I only change the thread on my machine when it runs out, so sometimes what is on there will match a make; other times, it will contrast. Both work for me. I love to see the stitches on something homemade and rough edges on fabric. I love a fraying hem on something hand-crafted. It saves time and effort, but it looks stylish, too.

Happy making.

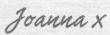

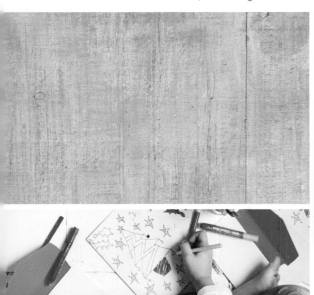

'Any parent knows that children love making things and they can surprise you with where their imaginations will lead them.'

by
KIDS

finger knitting

Finger knitting is a good precursor to knitting. It simply involves wrapping two bands of wool around a finger and pulling one loop over the other. Plus, it's super quick to produce reams of knitted lengths that can be turned into something lovely. It's very calming to be doing something that demands just enough attention to absorb you and clear your mind, but that doesn't require any real skill or hard concentration.

You can use any sort of wool or string, or even strips of fabric, for finger knitting. Be as creative as you like. As with any knitting, though, remember – chunky wool can be the most satisfying thing to work with, because it grows more quickly.

Uses for finger-knitted lengths

● *An alternative to ribbons — and they're edgier!*

● *You can tie finger-knitted bows onto anything to make it prettier: a ponytail, bag strap, plain hair grip, door handle, a set of keys...*

● *Or use a finger-knitted length to prettify and personalise a gift. You could use it to tie a bunch of flowers together, or tie one around a jam jar with flowers in, or to finish off a wrapped present. Or use it to tie up party balloons.*

● *Short lengths of finger knitting make lovely friendship bracelets. Tie one around your own wrist or ankle, and make them as presents for your friends, too.*

● *Keep a jar full of a variety of finger-knitted lengths. They're cheaper than ribbon and really cute.*

method

1 Leave a loose tail about 10cm long at the start of the ball of wool. Make a slip knot. Put this loose knot over the forefinger of your non-dominant hand and tighten, so that the loop is wound around the last joint of your finger, near to the nail. Grip the loose tail of wool between the other fingers on the same hand to anchor the loop in place.

2 Wind the ball end of wool around the forefinger, wrapping from the front of the finger over to the back, making a second loop about 5mm from the first, closer to the nail.

3 Slightly loosen the first loop, then use the fingers of your other hand to pull it over the second loop, keeping the second loop on your finger.

4 Tighten the stitch by pulling the forefinger away from the knot and pulling the ball end of the wool away from the work, towards yourself. Keep the loose end of the wool gripped under the other fingers while you pull, to anchor it. It's up to you how tight or loose you make the knotted stitches.

5 Reset by pushing the loop down the finger, back to the joint. Repeat these 4 steps, continuing until the finger knitting has reached the required length.

6 Cut the wool, leaving a 10cm loose end. Take the loop off your finger and pass the loose end through the loop. Pull tight to make a knot.

7 To finish off, hide the loose ends. Thread 1 onto a darning needle and weave it into the knitted length. Repeat with the other loose end – or use it to attach the finger-knitted length to something.

finger-knitted flowers

With a few twists and some stitches, a finger-knitted length can be transformed into a simple flower. Turn these into sweet hair accessories (stitch one onto a metal hair clip) or use them as embellishments for anything knitted. Or how about making the super-sweet flower garland below?

You can use different coloured wool for the petals and flower centre. Just knit an extra 3cm length as the centre in a contrasting colour.

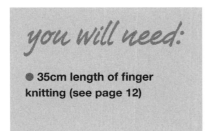

you will need:

● **35cm length of finger knitting (see page 12)**

method

1 Pinch a loop at the start of the length. Use a needle and thread to fix it with a couple of little stitches at the base of the loop. Pinch another loop, next to the first. Again, use a couple of stitches to secure it to the first loop, at the point at which the first loop was secured. Keep going until you have made 6 loops, working around a central point at which they are all secured.

2 Now wind the rest of the finger-knitted length in a spiral into the centre of the petals. Secure with little stitches as you go.

3 Use a needle to push the loose end of the wool through to the underside of the flower. Finish off by knotting the 2 ends together.

finger-knitted flower garland

Get everyone to muck in with the finger-knitted lengths for making flowers, and this can be a lovely collaborative project.

you will need:

● **12 finger-knitted flowers**

● **1.5m length of finger knitting (see page 12)**

method

Sew the first flower or to the knitted length, 15cm in from the end. Sew on the remaining flowers, spacing them 10cm apart.

pompoms simple style

Forget the traditional method of making pompoms, involving two cardboard rings – this is so much simpler and quicker. A child of any age with basic dexterity can make these. There is something very satisfying about making pompoms. There's no skill or effort required, just a lot of winding, a few quick snips and, hey presto – a crazy ball of fluff.

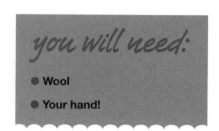

you will need:

● **Wool**

● **Your hand!**

method

1 Your hand is the perfect tool for making pompoms – you don't need to faff with cutting out any cardboard discs, and you can vary the size of the pompoms just by choosing whether to wrap wool around 2, 3 or 4 fingers. Keep your middle finger and forefinger together on your left hand (or right hand, if you are left-handed), for a small pompom. For a slightly larger one, hold the ring finger together with the others. And for a bigger one still, hold the little finger together as well. Ensure you hold the fingers slightly apart, so that they don't get bound together too tightly and go blue when the wool is being wound around. Now wind wool around the fingers again and again.

2 Continue to wind until a thick wodge of overlapped strands has built up; 50–100 winds should do it. The thicker the wodge, the better, as it will make for a chunkier pompom.

3 Cut a couple of 40cm lengths of wool. Carefully slide the looped wool off your fingers and hold it so that the loops stay together. Wind 1 of the 40cm strands around the centre of the loops a couple of times and pull each end tight so that the looped wool is cinched together in the middle, like a tight belt around a waist. Knot it as tightly as you can.

4 Use the second cut length of wool to tie the strands together in the middle again. The reason for doing it twice is because you will probably be able to pull this second piece tighter than the first, to ensure the cut wool in the pompom is securely held and doesn't fall out.

5 & 6 The tied loops will fan out into a circle. Cut through the looped wool. The ends will ping out instantly to create a ball.

7 Fluff up the ball by rubbing it between your hands.

8 Trim the pompom to shape.

note *To make a really big pompom, cut out a square of card, or use a small book to wind the wool around. The radius of the pompom will be half the width of the card or book.*

pompom brooch

The simplest thing you can make with a pompom is a funky brooch. Simply attach it to something with a safety pin. They look great on everything from T-shirts and tops to bags and coats. Multi-coloured pompoms work really well for this. Just change colours as you wind the wool around your hand.

pompom garland

This is a perfect rainy day project. Everyone can pile on the sofa, watch a movie and churn these out, or sit around the table together, making and talking. My idea of heaven – cosy companionship in crafting.

you will need:

- 15 pompoms of various colours and sizes (see page 18)
- Wool

method

Once you've gathered all the pompoms, use a large needle to thread them onto a 3m length of wool. Now you'll just have to fight over whose room it goes into. Or make another…

tip Keep all the pompom trimmings in a bag — they make great stuffing for little knitted toys (see the Monkey Bear on page 32).

knitting basics

As a child, I learned how to knit at school. Sadly, along with skills such as sewing and cooking, knitting has fallen off the national school curriculum in Britain. I am so passionate about these basic skills. They are probably as useful as the core subjects further down the track when you think about domestic life. I would love to see them reinstated in primary schools.

But it's not just because craft skills are useful in the practical 'how to' sense. Doing something creative with your hands is restorative. It creates time for the brain and body just to be, alert to nothing but the simple task in hand. As sleeping soothes and replenishes the mind and body, I really believe that spending a little time in a busy day quietly absorbed in the process of making has a similar effect.

So, if schools won't teach our children knitting, we parents should! And I don't just mean the girls. Boys can knit, too. Obviously not everyone will like it but, for some, it will be a skill for life.

The most off-putting thing about knitting can be the prospect of having to follow a complicated pattern. I knit loads of different things, but get around the issue of patterns by making everything out of simple squares or rectangles. It means you really don't need to know anything beyond the basics of knitting to produce something glorious.

Casting on
Make a slip knot in the wool, leaving a tail of about 10cm. Put the loop onto one of the needles and pull it so it is snug. Pick up the needle in your left hand. Hold the loose end of the wool against the needle to keep it out of the way. Hold the other needle in your right hand. Insert the right needle up through the bottom of the stitch on the left needle and to the back of the left needle, making a cross with the needles. Now loop the working yarn (from the ball) anticlockwise around the right needle and bring it forwards between the 2 needles. Hold the yarn firmly against the right needle and gently slide the right needle through the top of the slip knot on the left needle and under towards the front of the left needle, pulling the yarn you wrapped around it through the loop. Transfer the loop onto the left needle and gently pull it tight (but not too tight – the stitches need to be able to slide). That's it! First 2 stitches cast on. Working into the first stitch (the one nearest the tip) on the left needle, repeat until you've done as many as you need.

Knit stitch
Start exactly as you do with casting on, but when you get to the bit where the right needle passes through the wool that's been wound around, don't pull a loop to place onto the left needle, but keep the loop snugly on the right needle and slip the original stitch off the left needle. When you knit a stitch, the working yarn always stays at the back of the right needle.

Purl stitch
This is effectively a reverse of the knit stitch. With the yarn at the front of the right needle, insert the right needle down through the top of the first stitch on the left needle and to the front, making a cross with the needles. Loop the wool around the back of the right needle, so that it passes through the 2 needles. Holding the wool firmly against the right needle, gently slide the right needle down through the bottom of the loop on the left needle and back behind the left needle, pulling the yarn you wrapped around the right needle through the loop. Pull the working yarn tight and

slip the original stitch off the left needle. When you purl, the working yarn stays at the front of the right needle. Mixing knit and purl, you can create all sorts of patterns!

Casting off

Knit 2 stitches onto the right needle, then use the tip of the left needle to pick up the first stitch on the right needle. Carry this stitch over the second knitted stitch on the right needle and off the needle. Knit another stitch and repeat, pulling the first stitch over the second one and so on. When you have 1 stitch remaining on the right needle, just cut the wool to leave a tail of about 10cm. Slip the stitch off the needle and pass the end of the yarn through the last stitch and pull tightly.

Finishing loose ends

When you've got to the end of your knitting, the prospect of tidying up the loose ends seems like a hassle. It's one of those things that is more off-putting than it should be because, actually, it is very easy to do. It's also satisfying because, with very little effort, you can whittle away the ends and make them disappear so it looks like they were never there. Thread the loose end through a darning needle and weave it in and out of the backs of the stitches. The easiest way to do it is to run the needle in and around stitches and then pull the thread through all at once. It's best to weave ends through along the edges of the knitting, but if you have to weave across through the pattern, it's not disastrous. By echoing the stitches you should still be able to make the ends completely disappear.

tip *If you make a small mistake, don't panic! It's very easy to undo. Carefully take the last stitch off the needle and gently pull the long yarn back through the loop to undo the stitch — it will leave the loop of the previous stitch. Thread that carefully onto the left-hand needle. Undo as many as you need to correct your mistakes and then start knitting again. If the needle won't go back into the stitch easily when you're reknitting it, you've put it on the left-hand needle the wrong way around. Just hook it off carefully with the tip of the right-hand needle, half turn it and put it back on the left-hand needle, then knit. For more dramatic mistakes, see the tip on page 25.*

knitting basics continued

CHANGING WOOL

You'll need to do this when your ball of wool runs out, or if you want to change colours. If you can, it is best to change wool at the start or end of a row, so you don't have to worry about accidentally pulling the knot through a stitch. It's not disastrous if you suddenly find you need to change yarn halfway along a row, but try to make sure the knot pulls all the way through the stitches, or it will leave a hole where the wool hasn't pulled tight. Whenever you change wool, leave long (10cm) ends that can be woven in. To change wool, leave at least 20cm of wool at the end of your last row, use a loose knot to tie the new wool or colour around the loose end, then slide the knot up to the knitting and tighten it. Use the new yarn to make the first stitch in the next row.

Note: I have used Rowan Cocoon Wool for all the knitted projects in this book, but don't worry about using whatever wool you have. Any chunky wool will be great.

tip *For a video on how to knit, go to joannagosling.com*

For a strong finish, pull a needle length through, tie a slip knot, pull another needle length through, knot, pull through a few more stitches and trim. Whether or not you need a strong finish depends on what you're making. I do it on things that need to be hardwearing, such as scarves, but on most other things a length simply woven through should suffice.

Buying wool

A quick word on buying wool: beware – it can be very expensive. I had this idea of only knitting butter-soft, beautifully coloured cashmere – until I discovered the crazy cost of buying it. My tip for a great alternative is 100% alpaca, or a mix of fibres, which is just as gorgeous and supersoft, but much better value. It is not cheap buying any good-quality wool, but I would say, if you are taking the time to knit something that will hopefully last forever, it is worth buying the best, softest wool you can afford.

If you are buying in skeins, you'll need to roll it into balls before you start knitting with it, or it will just end up in a tangled, frustrating mess of knots. Done that. Trust me, it's a cut corner that wastes a lot more time and effort in the long run. Some shops have a machine to ball wool when you buy it, so don't forget to ask. If you have to do it yourself, the easiest way I've found is to forget getting someone to hold the loops around their arms; just do it yourself with the loops around your ankles. Carefully unwind the twisted skein so that it is one big loop. Either untie or snip the threads holding the strands of wool together. Put your feet up on the sofa and put the loop over your ankles. Stretch out so the wool is taut. Now just unravel at your own pace, winding the wool into a ball as you go.

Before you start

Before you crack on, don't plunge straight into a project. Practise by casting on 8 stitches and knitting 8 rows a few times. It'll take a little while to get the hang of the tension. It's not difficult, but you just need to get the feel of it. The first couple of rows will always feel stiff, but the tension eases off once you get into your third row, which makes the knitting much easier and smoother. It's also a good idea to keep checking the number of stitches on the needle while you're practising, because it's very easy to accidentally add extra stitches, or drop some, when you're starting out. Stitches get added when you accidentally hook an extra loop when you pass the right-hand needle through the loop on the left, so you just need to watch that carefully at the start.

Happy knitting!

teddy bear scarf

A knitted teddy bear scarf is a perfect starter project for a young beginner knitter as it's small, simple and quick, and is actually useful – or, at least, there is a use for it that any teddy owner will find pleasing. So churn out as many of these as you like while mastering the joyous art of knitting, and dress up your own teddies. Wrap up spares as presents for friends. How about a matching 'friendship' pair for yours and your best friend's teddies?

you will need:

● Size 6.5mm needles

● Chunky wool

method

1 Leave a loose end of about 10cm. Cast on 5 stitches. Knit 70 rows. Cast off, leaving a loose end of about 10cm.

2 Weave 1 of the loose ends through the end of the scarf and pull it tight so that that end is bunched together into a point. Repeat on the other end. Leave the loose ends long to use for sewing on the pompoms.

3 Make 2 small pompoms (see page 18), winding the wool around 2 fingers about 40 times. Trim each pompom well to ensure both are of the same size.

4 Sew 1 pompom onto 1 end of the scarf using the loose end of wool. Repeat with the other pompom on the opposite end of the scarf.

tip *In the event of a knitting catastrophe — wrong stitches, or the needle slips clean out of the knitting — stay calm. Lay the knitting flat on a surface and remove both needles. Pull the loose end gently to undo as many rows as necessary to get you back to the pre-mistake point. It will reveal a line of perfect loops. Carefully slot one needle through all except the last loop, where the loose end of yarn is. You will see the loose end is between the last stitch and the penultimate one. Put this last stitch on the other needle and knit as though you were finishing the row — this the last stitch. That's it. You can carry on knitting as normal.*

knitted bow

This small, sweet frippery can be knitted very quickly and used to jazz up clothes and hats, or can be given as presents to friends.

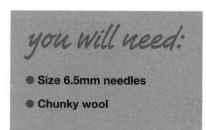

you will need:

- Size 6.5mm needles
- Chunky wool
- Safety pin

method

1 Cast on 8 stitches. Knit 40 rows. Cast off.

2 Fold the piece in half across the length to make a rectangle. Use the loose ends to sew the 2 short ends together. (There's no need to sew all the way around.)

3 Cut a 50cm length of wool. Tie it round the middle of the rectangle, pulling it tightly together. Wind all the wool around the centre and knot it at the back.

4 Slide the safety pin under the wound wool at the back of the bow. It is now ready to pin anywhere you like.

knitted tie

A great project for a boy to make: an old fashioned tie that looks funky in its retro style.

you will need:

- Size 6.5mm needles
- Chunky wool

method

Cast on 6 stitches. Knit 140 rows. Cast off. Tie on. Simple. It might be a bit tricky to do up at first as it won't slide very easily. Knot the tie and undo the knot a few times, trying to slide it each time. After a few goes the tie will have stretched out enough and will work a treat.

note *How about a matching tie for Daddy? Cast on 9 stitches and knit 165 rows.*

pompom phone case

Once you get your hands on your first grown-up pride-and-joy possession, the next thing is to ensure you keep hold of it... which is where this phone case comes in. It's perfect for slinging the mobile around a neck, across the body or on a peg. It makes a great present, plus it's a really quick and easy knit, which makes it another great starter project for a beginner knitter.

you will need:

● Size 6.5mm needles
● Chunky wool

method

1 Leaving a 40cm loose end, cast on 8 stitches. Knit 55 rows. Cast off.

2 Fold the knitted rectangle in half across the length to make a pouch. Use the loose ends to sew the sides of the pouch together. Turn the pouch the right way out.

3 To make the strap, finger knit (see page 12) an 80cm length, leaving long, loose ends.

4 Feed 1 end of the finger-knitted length through a gap in the stitches on 1 side of the opening of the pouch, at the seam, then weave it back out through another gap a couple of stitches along. Knot to anchor the strap in place, leaving a 5cm length of finger knitting dangling loose. Repeat on the opposite side of the pouch with the other end of the finger-knitted strap.

5 Make 2 small pompoms (see page 18). Tie 1 onto the end of 1 strap using the loose end of the finger knitting. Repeat with the other pompom on the other end of the strap.

pompom scarf

Once the mini teddy bear scarf has been mastered, stepping up to a kid-sized scarf requires no extra skill. Obviously, it does require more patience, as a bigger project takes more time to make. It uses the same basic knit stitch as the teddy scarf, only on a bigger scale. So I've scaled up the size of the needles to make the job a little quicker.

you will need:

- **Size 8mm needles**
- **200g chunky wool**
- **Enough extra wool to make 2 giant pompoms (in the same colour as the scarf or a contrasting one)**

method

1 Cast on 20 stitches, leaving a long tail. Knit 200 rows or thereabouts – the scarf should be about 140cm long. Cast off, leaving a long tail.

2 Make 2 pompoms (see page 18). To make oversized pompoms, wind the wool around a 15cm-wide piece of card instead of your hand, using exactly the same method. To make the pompom super chunky you will need to wind the wool around about 200 times!

3 Gather 1 end of the scarf so that it is cinched into a point, at which a pompom can be sewn on. To do this, thread the loose tail onto a darning needle.

4 Weave it along the short edge of the scarf then pull it – the end of the scarf will concertina. Thread the tail back through the gathered end and secure the gather with a knot. Now stitch the pompom onto the point. Repeat with the other pompom at the other end of the scarf.

pompom hat

I love this hat. It's just glorious, but all you need to be able to do to make it is knit a basic rectangle. It's so simple to make and it looks totally gorgeous with the pompom scarf on page 29. It also makes a fabulous present.

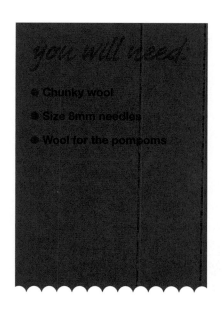

you will need

- Chunky wool
- Size 8mm needles
- Wool for the pompoms

method

1 Cast on 20 stitches. Knit 80 rows. You should have a rectangle measuring approximately 19 x 30cm. This will make a hat to fit a 5-year-old and onwards (it fits me, too, and I don't have a particularly dainty head!).

2 Fold the rectangle in half lengthways to make a folded rectangle measuring about 19 x 15cm.

3 Sew 1 side seam together, sewing a curve at the top that will create a rounded edge instead of a right angle when it's turned the right way out.

4 Repeat on the other side (see diagram).

5 Flip the hat inside out, so that the seams are on the inside. Make 2 chunky pompoms (see page 18) using 3 or 4 fingers. Sew a pompom onto each top corner of the hat. The hat can be worn whichever way you like – with the pompoms at the front and back of your head, or at the sides like cute antennae.

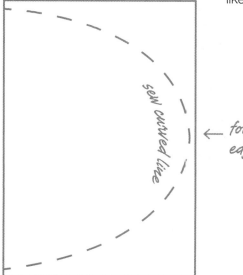

sew curved line

← folded edge

knitted monkey bear

I call this a monkey bear because it resembles a cute little hybrid of the two. Actually, it looks a bit like a cat, too. Or even a rabbit – to turn him into one, just make the ears a bit longer. The point is, you can churn out a few simple knitted rectangles and transform them into a cute, cuddly creature. This is one of those the-sum-is-greater-than-its-parts classics.

you will need:

- Size 6.5mm needles
- Chunky wool in main colour
- Small amount of chunky wool in a paler contrasting colour to the main colour (optional) for the face
- Small amount of chunky wool in a darker contrasting colour to the main colour (optional) for the eyes and nose
- Stuffing (leftover wool is perfect, or use pompom trimmings – see page 21)

method

1 You need to knit 7 rectangles of different sizes – 1 for the head, 2 body pieces, 2 arms and 2 legs. Leave extra-long loose tails of about 30cm on each of the rectangles to use for sewing the pieces together.

Arms (make 2)
Cast on 16 stitches. Knit 10 rows. Cast off.
Legs (make 2)
Cast on 20 stitches. Knit 10 rows. Cast off.
Body (make 2)
Cast on 20 stitches. Knit 26 rows. Cast off.
Head
Cast on 20 stitches. Knit 40 rows. Cast off.

Sew the arms and legs
2 To turn the arm and leg rectangles into Monkey Bear parts, fold each one in half lengthways and sew the long edge together using a long loose tail. Now sew 1 short end together, working a curve shape around the 2 corners – don't sew right to the end, but shape the stitches around in a curve to cut off the corners. Turn the tube inside out through the open end so that the stitches are on the inside. You will see that the sewn end is rounded, for the paw.

Sew the body
3 Align the 2 body pieces one on top of the other. To sew the arms into the body, sandwich them in between the large knitted rectangles, about 4cm from the top of the rectangle with the arms on the inside of the rectangle, and with the open ends just sticking out of the edges. Fix them in place by sewing them into the side seams of the body. When you reach the bottom of the rectangle, round off the corners as you did with the hands and feet, to create a soft curve at the bottom of the body. Position the legs in the same way as you did the arms, so that they are sandwiched inside the body, with the open ends caught in the seam. When positioning the legs,

leave a gap of about 2cm between them. Once the arms and legs are sewn in, finish off the top of the body by sewing a curved seam for the shoulders, just above the arms. Leave a 5cm gap open at the neck.

4 Turn the body the right way out so the arms and legs are on the outside. Stuff the body, but don't overfill it.

Sew the head
5 To make the head, fold the rectangle in half with the knitting weave running the same way as that on the body. Sew the 2 side edges together, curving your stitches in a circular shape, and stitching 2 ear shapes at the top. Leave a gap of 4cm open at the base. Turn the head right side out, then push the ears out. Lightly stuff the head. Gather the bottom of the head together (but not too tightly), to shape it, then stitch it closed.

Sew together
6 Sew the head onto the body. Don't worry about making your stitches neat. The beauty of sewing knitted pieces together with the wool used to make the pieces is that your stitches are invisible.

Make a tail
7 Now for the tail. Using the main colour, double finger knit a 20cm length (see note on left). Thread 1 loose end into a darning needle and push it through the back of the body in the position at which you want the tail. Make the tail as short as you like by pushing excess length inside the body. Secure with several stitches. To hide the loose end at the end of the tail, thread it up through the inside of the tail and into the body.

Hello Monkey Bear! I love him plain like this, even without a face. You can leave him just as he is or embellish him however you like.

Make a face
8 It's quite nice to make a face in a contrasting colour, like the face of a real monkey. If you want to do that, knit another rectangle using the paler contrasting colour. Cast on 10 stitches. Knit 10 rows. Cast off.

9 Sew the face onto the head, shaping it slightly as you go (just push the edges under to shape) so that it is rounded and narrower at the top. Before finishing the sewing, push a little stuffing under the face to pad it a bit. Sew on the eyes and mouth with a few stitches in a darker colour.

note *Double finger knitting is very similar to normal finger knitting (see page 12). Start with a loop on your index finger, as with single finger knitting, then wind the wool over and under your middle finger, then back over and under your index finger, and then over and under your middle finger again so that you have 2 loops on each finger. Pull the first loop through the second loop on each finger and continue. If this sounds a bit confusing, there's a 'how to' video at joannagosling.com*

note *Monkey Bear looks great in a Teddy Bear Scarf (see page 25)*

knitted headband

This rolls up small, so it can be stashed in a pocket or school bag ready to be retrieved whenever the temperature dips. To make one, simply knit a narrow rectangle. It's a satisfying, easy project for kids, but they're great presents for grown-ups to knit for kids, too.

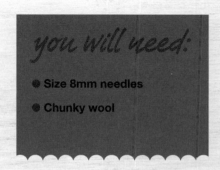

you will need:

● **Size 8mm needles**
● **Chunky wool**

method

1 Leaving a 15cm loose tail, cast on 12 stitches. Knit 75 rows. Cast off, leaving a long tail.

2 Thread both loose ends through the large eye of a darning needle and sew the short ends of the rectangle together. Weave the loose tails through the stitches for a neat finish.

note *A giant finger-knitted flower (see page 17) or a pompom (see page 18) would look great stitched onto the headband.*

legwarmers/boot liners

Depending on whether these are being knitted by or for a boy or a girl, they can be called boot liners or legwarmers. Either way, they do the same trick – they keep the legs extra-toasty in wintertime while looking pretty funky. They are made with a contrasting band of colour at the tops. You could reverse the colours, or make them completely mismatched. Again, these are just made from a knitted rectangle – but this time, you need to add in a purl stitch (see page 22).

you will need:

- Size 8mm needles
- 100g chunky wool
- 40g chunky wool in a contrasting colour

method

1 Cast on 28 stitches. Instead of doing simple knit stitch all the way, alternate 2 knit and 2 purl stitches. This creates a chunky, extra-cosy rib that will stretch to fit all sizes.

2 Knit 52 rows, alternating 2 knit and 2 purl stitches.

3 Change colour (see page 24) and knit another 8 rows, continuing with the 2 knit, 2 purl rib pattern.

4 Cast off.

5 Repeat to make an identical knitted rectangle.

6 Fold the rectangle in half across the width. Sew the long side edges together to create a tube, but leave the edges of the contrasting colour band at the top unsewn.

7 Repeat with the second knitted rectangle. Put these on with the contrasting band at the top, and fold the bands over the top of a boot.

sewing machine basics

I would recommend you buy a basic regular sewing machine as a child's first machine, rather than one specifically marketed for children. It can be tempting to go for something that's been prettified with kids in mind, but the most important thing is that it actually does the job effectively, or else a child will just become frustrated. My experience of kid-specific machines has been that the stitches just unravel or the machine doesn't last for long. I figure you can't go wrong with something designed for longevity, not as a child's toy. A good basic sewing machine should be a trusty tool to last into adulthood.

Learning how to use a sewing machine is liberating for a young creative mind. How great it is to be able to make something you've designed in your own head! Obviously, things can be hand-sewn, but machine-stitching is so much quicker and really not difficult at all.

At first, the speed of the needle whizzing away can be daunting. It's important to never forget that you're in control of the machine, not the other way round. A good way to get used to the way a machine works – to feel comfortable with it and learn how to control it – is to ignore the foot pedal at first. Just use the hand wheel to stitch mechanically, albeit slowly.

sewing machine tips

● Before operating the foot pedal, make sure the feet (the split plate at the base of the needle that goes up and down by moving a lever) are down to hold the fabric in place, and that the needle is pushed down into the fabric, into the position where you want to start sewing.

● Use the hand wheel to move the needle manually when inserting the needle into the fabric, so that you can carefully control where it goes in.

● Press your hands firmly but gently onto the fabric to guide it through as the needle zips in and out, keeping your fingers pressed together, but your hands out of the path of the needle. You can shift the direction of the stitches or create a curved edge by moving the fabric as you go.

● If you need to completely change the direction of the stitches, ensure the needle is pushed down into the fabric, then lift the feet and turn the fabric until the feet are pointing in the direction in which you want your stitches to go. Lower the feet again and continue sewing.

● If you want a strong seam (for instance, when making a bag that might carry heavy loads), set the stitch length to 2 for short stitches that will hold the seams together tightly. Shorter stitches can be difficult to unpick, so I generally use a default stitch length setting of 3–4 for most things as it can be unpicked very easily in the event of a mistake. If you do need to unpick any stitches, the easiest way is to use a seam ripper.

● You can reinforce the stitches at the start and end by oversewing. Just push the lever that reverses the direction of sewing. Sew a few stitches backwards. Release the lever and sew forwards again.

● When detaching your project from the machine, manually raise the needle to its highest point. Pull the fabric away until there is about 10cm of thread between the fabric and the machine. Cut the threads at the midway point. This will mean they are long enough to knot easily on the fabric, and also long enough not to come unthreaded on the machine. Pull the top thread and bobbin thread on the machine out past the back of the needle ready for next time.

● The easiest way to knot the loose ends is to pull one of them to loosen the last stitch, creating a loop as the loose end from the other side of the fabric starts to come through. Pull it through, knot the two ends together and trim. If the stitches are too tight, thread one of the ends onto a needle to push it through to the other side before knotting.

bobbin winder

thread guide

bobbin winder
tension disc

spool pins

take up
lever

stitch selector

stitch length dial

hand wheel

lever to lift feet
(other side)

reverse stitch lever

feet

needle

needle plate (this
part pulls away to
access the bobbin)

magnetic pin jar

I use my old upcycling favourite, a jam jar, for this project. Magnets are so practical for catching the fiddly bits and bobs used for sewing. Scrabbling around for a needle I could have sworn I'd left on my desk used to drive me mad! So now I have a couple of magnets stuck to my sewing desk lamp. The magnetic pin jar is just an extension of that. It's quicker and easier to make than a pincushion and just brilliant to use when you're removing pins as you sew – absent-mindedly dangle them in the direction of your magnetic pin jar and it will gobble them up so you don't end up with pins scattered all over the table or on the floor.

As a guide, I use 6mm diameter disc magnets that are 1mm thick, just because I buy them in bulk to use for everything I make using magnets. This size is a great all-rounder. But I don't want to be prescriptive about the sort of magnet as it really doesn't matter – any type will do the job.

method

1 Fix the magnets to the underside of the lid. You don't need glue – they will stick on the metal by attraction. Position them across the lid to increase the magnetic area.

2 Cover the top and the sides of the jar lid in double-sided tape. Peel off the tape backing, stick your scrap of fabric to the tape and cut it to size.

3 For a neat finish, cover the underside of the jar lid too. Cut a disc of fabric to size and cover it with double-sided tape. Peel off the tape backing and stick it onto the underside of the lid.

4 Fill the jar with pins and put extras on the lid for easy access when you are sewing.

you will need:

● **Jam jar with a metal lid**

● **2–3 small magnets**

● **Double-sided tape**

● **Scrap of fabric**

note *If you've dropped any pins on the floor while sewing, just waft the jar over the area and it will pick them up like a vacuum cleaner.*

sewing machine cover

Most sewing machines come with a very unappealing white plastic cover to protect them when not in use. Personally, I love to see a sewing machine on display, as I think they are gorgeous bits of kit, so I never use the ugly plastic cover to hide mine. The only thing is that they can get dusty, so it is a good idea to keep your machine covered if it's not in use for a while. So, a good first sewing project is to make your own lovely cover that is nice to look at.

you will need:

- 0.5m fabric (oil cloth is best, if you can get it)
- Plastic cover that came with the machine
- Craft knife

method

1 Cut the plastic cover into the three sections that were sewn together to make it (2 sides and 1 long strip for the top and narrower sides). You'll use these pieces as your templates for the new, improved version.

2 Pin 1 of the side pieces onto the new fabric. Cut around, adding an extra 1.5cm margin around 3 of the sides (the 2 shorter ends and the top) to allow for a seam when you sew the pieces together. Cut a second piece the same size. Pin the long strip onto the fabric. Cut out, adding an extra 1.5cm margin along the long sides for the seam allowance.

3 Pin the long strip onto 1 of the side pieces with the right sides facing in. Starting at 1 of the short edges, pin along the top side of the cover, then back down the second short edge. Leaving a 1cm seam allowance, machine stitch around the 3 sides. Repeat with the second side piece of fabric to complete the cover.

4 Flip the cover so that the right sides are facing out. Place it over the sewing machine. With the cover on, lift up the carry handle on the top of the machine and position the cover so that the handle is centred on the top section. Use a craft knife to cut a slit through the fabric, along the middle of where the handle touches the fabric. If you have used oil cloth, there's no need to worry about fraying, because the raw edges won't unravel at all. If you've used regular fabric, I'd still not worry about fraying. This is a quick and easy, minimum effort, maximum return make – rough edges are all part of the appeal!

simple bag

Bags are a very satisfying thing to make – both for yourself and to give as a gift – because they are easy to create and always useful.

you will need:

• Fabric measuring 75 x 27cm

• 2 smaller pieces of fabric, each measuring 75 x 7cm

---

note *This bag is perfect for books, swimming stuff, PE kit, toys or for taking on a journey. It's also a great gift to make for a grown up.*

method

1 Fold the large piece of fabric in half widthways to make a rectangle measuring 37.5 x 27cm, with the right side facing in. Sew down each side, leaving a 1cm seam allowance. Use a small stitch setting on the machine for strength.

2 Fold over the top of the bag twice to make a hem with the raw edge folded inside. Make the first fold 1cm deep, then fold over the hem again by 2cm. Sew all the way around, close to the fold.

3 Now make the bag straps. Fold 1 of the long strips of fabric in half lengthways with the right side facing in. Sew around the long edge and 1 of the short ends, leaving a 0.5cm seam allowance.

4 To turn the tube the right way out, push the pointed end of a chopstick or knitting needle into the short stitched end of the tube, pushing the end into the tube. Keep pushing the chopstick into the tube, taking the fabric with it, to eventually turn the tube the right way out, with the seams on the inside. If you can't grip the fabric easily to guide the chopstick in, lick your fingers and then it will work. Don't push too fast or you will end up with a bunched-up wodge of fabric that won't budge. The chopstick should glide in fairly easily if you do it right. When the strap is turned the right way out, fold in the open end of the strap and stitch it together. Press flat. Repeat to make the second strap.

5 Pin 1 strap onto the top hem of the bag, about 4cm in from the side seam. Pin the other end of the strap on the opposite edge of the same side of the bag, ensuring it is not twisted. Repeat with the second strap.

6 Ensure you are happy with the positions of the straps, then sew each of the 4 ends of the strap onto the bag hem.

7 Stitch the outline of a square onto the end of each bag strap, covering the area that's attached to the bag hem, for extra strength.

8 Finally, press the bag so that the edges are all crisp.

festival bag

I designed this bag for a sewing party my eldest daughter was having for her eleventh birthday. I wanted her guests to be able to make something quick and simple but really funky that would be a great souvenir of a special day. It got dubbed the Festival Bag by one of the girls because of the boho style.

Making these bags uses my absolutely favourite trick of making a lined bag in a few easy steps. It's so simple and looks really neat and professional.

you will need:

● 4 pieces of fabric, each measuring 35 x 25cm (use 2 different fabrics so you have 2 rectangles of each)

● 2 x 35cm lengths of pompom trim

● 1m length of wide ribbon

method

1 Align 2 matching pieces of fabric with the right sides facing in. Fold the top shorter edge down and outwards to make a hem. Pin to hold the hem in place. Repeat with the other 2 matching pieces of fabric.

2 Align the fabric rectangles together, 1 joined pair on top of the other. Sew around 3 sides of the bag, allowing for a 1cm seam, leaving the folded top edges open.

3 Now for the magic! Holding 3 pieces of fabric together, flip the bag inside out. Now flip it inside out again, this time 2 pieces of fabric together in each hand. You can flip it inside out again if you like, depending on which fabric you want as lining and which you want on the outside.

4 Slip the lengths of pompom trim between the folded hems at the top of the bag, working your way around the bag opening. Ensure the edging is hidden and the pompoms stick out. Pin the pompom trim in place.

5 Fold over the top of the bag outwards so that you have a 5cm band of the lining showing on the outside, with the pompoms hanging down from it. Machine-stitch this folded band all the way around the bag, ensuring you sew through the pompom edging to secure it in place.

6 Now sew on the ribbon cross-body strap. Fold over 1 end of the ribbon towards the wrong side a couple of times before sewing, to stop the end fraying. Repeat on the other end of the strap.

7 Pin each end of the strap onto the outside of the bag on opposite sides of the bag, at the side seams. Adjust the length as required. Sew on the 2 ends of the strap, using a short stitch length, sewing back and forth over each end several times for added strength.

butterfly bracelet

This bracelet costs almost nothing to make but looks as if it comes from a gorgeous boutique. There is one specific piece of kit you need for these – a little butterfly punch, or two, if you want butterflies of different sizes. We use them a lot for making little embellishments for various projects, so they're a worthwhile investment and they're not expensive. You can also use a regular hole punch to create round tin sequins, which are just as lovely.

Tonic Studios make a range of metal punches. Search for them online.

you will need:

- **Butterfly punch or hole punch**
- **Metal salvaged from an empty drinks can (see note on page 50)**
- **Thick fabric (such as felt, denim or linen)**
- **Popper snap**

method

1 Cut the fabric to size. As you can see from the picture, there's no need to worry about being precise about the dimensions. I suggest 16 x 1cm, but you can make it narrower or wider if you prefer, and longer if you need. Felt is perfect for this project as it won't fray at all. Other fabrics will fray slightly, but that only adds to the charm.

2 Punch out your butterflies or sequins from the salvaged tin using the butterfly punch or hole punch.

3 This step should be left to the grown ups. To make a hole through the metal so that it can be sewn on, place the cut-out shape on a cushion or a sponge. Position a needle where you want the hole to be. Hold it carefully in place and use something hard (I use the flat bit of my punches), to press down into the metal. The needle will go through it pretty easily. You only need 1 hole through a sequin, but 2 or 4 on each butterfly, depending on their size.

4 Sew the shapes onto the wristband.

5 Sew each half of the popper onto the ends of the wristband, ensuring you've got them the right way around so that they will snap together.

tattooed tin can badges

The thin metal that fizzy drinks cans are made out of is a wonderful free gift for a crafter, and here's one way to use it – to make cute badges. They're simple to make, so this project is perfect for little ones.

Leave this bit to the grown ups: to salvage the metal from old drinks cans, pierce the container with a pair of scissors and cut around the top. Cut down the side to the bottom, then cut away the base, too. Bend and roll the metal in the opposite direction to the curve to flatten it out. You now have a rectangle of tin. Get into the habit of doing this with all your empty cans, to build up a little supply. Incidentally, cutting the tin will sharpen your scissors, so if you've got a blunt pair, this is a good way to revive them.

method

1 Fix a temporary tattoo to the plain side of the metal, in the same way you would apply it to the skin.

2 Carefully cut the metal around the shape of the tattoo.

3 To finish off, glue a badge pin on the back.

4 These are great on clothes or bags. And they make a lovely finishing touch to a wrapped parcel. Or pin one onto the front of a folded piece of extra-thick paper to make a greetings card. A more permanent way of enjoying temporary tattoos!

you will need:

● **Metal salvaged from an empty drinks can**

● **Temporary tattoos**

● **1 badge pin per badge**

● **Strong glue**

tip *Instead of using a temporary tattoo, you could cut a shape like a heart or a star and cover the metal with double-sided tape, then cover that with glitter for ultra glitzy style.*

bottle cap badges

My sister gave me a whole load of bottle caps, because her sons love collecting them, and asked me to work out how to turn them into badges. It took me a while as I was trying to think of a way of filling the deep gap on the back in order to attach a pin, and couldn't work out a simple way of doing it. Suddenly, the eureka moment hit. Magnets! So, this isn't really a make, but it is an ultra simple way of turning nice bottle caps into covetable badges.

you will need:

- 2 disc magnets (6mm in diameter and 1mm thick)
- 1 bottle top

method

Fix 1 of the magnets onto the underside of the bottle cap. Don't worry about gluing it – the magnetic force will fix it in place. Position it on the item you want to fix the badge onto, and hold the second magnet underneath the fabric. The magnets will pull together and fix the badge in place.

note *This project comes with a slight health warning – ensure the kids using these badges are old enough to understand that magnets mustn't be eaten!*

quill pen

Any Harry Potter fan will love this old-fashioned pen. It takes just a few seconds to make. The hardest part is finding the feather. But that's part of the fun of making – getting out and about to find your treasures.

You can buy giant feathers cheaply in craft shops if you have no luck finding any in the wild!

you will need:

● **Largest feather you can find**

● **Insert from a cheap biro**

● **Spray paint (optional)**

method

1 Cut off the tip of the feather shaft. Cut off a little bit at first. You can always cut off a little extra if you need to. You want to make an opening that is big enough to take the pen insert, but tight enough to keep it fixed in place.

2 The pen insert will probably be too long to fit into the feather, so you may need to trim it to size. Again, cut little by little, so you don't take too much off.

3 Push the pen insert into the shaft of the feather.

4 Finally, spray paint the feather, if you like, and leave to dry.

tip *An ultra cool alternative is to use the feather without a biro insert for writing secret messages with invisible ink. The best way I have found to do that is to use uncoloured glow-in-the-dark paint. Just dip the the quill in the luminous paint and write your note. Leave it to dry. To read it, go somewhere dark or hide under the bedcovers and the message will glow, like magic!*

homemade book

Children of all ages love little notebooks. Actually, who doesn't love a notebook? A private space to scribble down thoughts and pictures. Making them from scratch couldn't be easier and kids will be delighted by how simple it is to actually make their own book. Once they know how, I guarantee they'll be making them all the time, for themselves and their friends.

Use whatever papers you have to hand – white or coloured paper, newspaper, kraft paper, anything you like.

you will need:

● **Papers, all cut to a rectangle of the same size**

● **Needle and thread**

● **Fabric**

● **Double-sided tape**

method

1 Pile the paper together and cut if necessary so that all the pieces are the same shape and aligned. Fold the paper wodge in half to make the shape of a book.

2 Now use a needle and thread to sew the pages together through the fold. The first holes might be difficult to push through, even with something protecting your finger (see the tip box below). So, press the needle into the paper to fix it in position, then put the base of the needle on your table and press the paper down onto it firmly (get a grown-up to do this bit). Once the holes are made, it should be easy to sew through them. Oversew several times for strength.

3 Cover the outside sheet of paper in double-sided tape. Peel off the backing, then fix the fabric to the tape. Trim the fabric to size.

note
Use rubber stamps to print a title or pattern on the front cover. (See page 138 for how to make cork stamps.)

tip *I hate using thimbles because they hinder dexterity, so instead I use a scrap of leather positioned over the tip of the finger used to push the needle through the paper.*

i heart you t-shirt

Decorating a plain T-shirt is always a good rainy day activity – it's fun and creative, but you also get something to keep and use afterwards. It's always satisfying to wear your own creations. Sticky backed plastic is absolutely brilliant to use for fabric printing funky designs that look screen printed. To offer you a starting point, here is a design created by my middle daughter, but don't be constrained. You can do anything you like with this simple technique.

you will need:

- ● **Sticky backed plastic**
- ● **Craft knife**
- ● **T-shirt**
- ● **Sponge**
- ● **Fabric paint**

method

1 Draw a heart shape onto the shiny side of the sticky backed plastic. Use a craft knife to cut out the image and make a stencil.

2 Peel off the backing of the sticky backed plastic (keep the backing) and stick the stencil (the outline of the heart shape, not the cut-out piece itself) onto the fabric, ensuring both fabric and sticky backed plastic are completely smooth.

3 Place a sheet of kitchen foil or newspaper between the front and back layers of the T-shirt. This is to stop the paint leaching through the fabric onto the back.

4 Lightly sponge fabric paint into the cut out area of the stencil, building up a strong colour. Leave to dry.

5 Peel off the sticky backed plastic carefully. Stick it back onto its backing so you can reuse it.

6 Follow the fabric paint packet instructions to fix your design permanently onto the T-shirt fabric (normally, you have to iron over the design, with a cloth laid between the paint and the iron).

skipping elastic

You can buy a ready-made skipping elastic cheaply enough, but this one's worth making for its sheer prettiness and individuality. And it's a lovely thing to make and play with together at home. It's funny how the same simple rhymes and games pass down the generations as if by osmosis.

you will need:

● 3m piece of 1cm-wide elastic in any colour

● Scraps of ribbons and strips of fabric

method

1 Simply tie short lengths of ribbon and torn strips of fabric along the length of the elastic. You want it to look colourful and fun, but don't overdo it or the strips will get in the way of skipping.

2 Knot the ends of the elastic together with a secure double knot. Hours of free entertainment ahead!

plaited hairband

Sweet simplicity. Girls love to plait and making this cute hairband provides an opportunity for them to do just that.

you will need:

● 3 torn strips of fabric, each measuring 2cm x 1m

method

1 Hold the strips of fabric together and knot together at one end. Leave a 3cm gap, then make another knot.

2 Plait the strips together for 50cm. Knot.

3 To tie the hairband around the head, push the opposite end through the gap between the 2 knots you made at the beginning of the plait. Adjust the length to fit by pulling tight.

note *Push a few feathers through the plaited strips for funky Hiawatha style.*

bath bomb eggs

Hollowed eggs can be turned into beautiful bath bombs for an Easter gift. To use them, you put a whole egg in the bath and the bomb will gently fizz and slowly disperse through the hole. A box of these, finished with a pretty ribbon, looks gorgeous, but they are very simple for kids to make.

you will need:

- Box of 6 eggs (duck's or hen's)
- 300g bicarbonate of soda
- 150g cream of tartar
- 50g oats
- Approximately 10ml scent (little sample bottles come for free and are perfect) or essential oils
- 30ml almond oil
- Spray atomizer
- Ribbon or string

tip *You could decorate the shells with temporary tattoos (see the picture).*

method

1 First, prepare the eggshells. Use a pin to prick several holes into the base of an egg and gently push to make a hole that's large enough to fit your finger. Pour out the yolk and white through the hole. If they don't come out easily, poke a stick through the hole to break them up; they should then pour out easily. Repeat with the remaining eggs. Rinse the shells clean with plenty of water and leave to dry.

2 Combine the bicarbonate of soda, cream of tartar, oats, scent or essential oils and almond oil in a large mixing bowl. Scrunch them together using your hands, as if making dough. The mixture should come together in crumbly clumps when you press it.

3 You need to add a little water to get the ingredients to bind together properly and hold a shape, but if you use too much, the mixture will start to fizz and swell and you won't be able to make it into bombs. Use a spray atomiser to spritz the mix with 6 or 7 squirts of water. Press the mixture together until it binds but is still loose and crumbly as in the picture.

4 Now put the mix into the eggshells using your hands. Press the mixture down firmly in each shell using your finger. When the shell is full, wipe it clean and leave it to set. It takes about 24 hours for the mixture to become hard, but it doesn't really matter with these bath bomb eggs, as the shell holds them together.

5 Package up the eggs as a gift in the egg box. To prettify it, peel off the paper label on the outside of the box and use rubber stamps to print a message on the box lid. If the box has printing on it, cut out a piece of pretty paper and stick it on top. You could also line the insides with pretty fabric. Tie the box together with a piece of string or ribbon. To use the bath bomb eggs, simply drop one into a bath of water and enjoy!

chocolate eggs

These are really fun to make and eat because they use real eggshells. When you crack one open, it's filled with chocolate! They look great when wrapped individually in cellophane or packaged in a decorated egg box.

you will need:

● **Box of 6 eggs (hen's eggs are best; because they're brown, the chocolate won't show through)**

● **350g milk chocolate, chopped**

● **150ml double cream**

● **1 tablespoon cocoa powder**

● **Salt**

● **Plastic food bag**

tip *Wrap the eggs individually in cellophane, or package up in an egg box tied with a ribbon.*

method

1 Hollow out the eggs using the method described on page 60, so that you have empty shells with a single large hole in the base.

2 Melt 100g of the chocolate slowly and gently (this is so that it rehardens properly). Place it in a small bowl and set it over a pan of simmering water to make a bain marie. As soon as it starts to melt, stir it with a spatula until it is fully melted and runny. (You can also melt chocolate in the microwave, zapping it in short bursts of 25 seconds and stirring in between.)

3 Pour a dessertspoon or so of chocolate into an eggshell, letting it pour off the tip of the spoon. Roll the shell around so that the inside is completely coated. Add a little more chocolate if you need. Repeat with all the shells, let cool slightly, then put them in the fridge to allow the chocolate to set.

4 Heat 200g of the chocolate with the double cream in a saucepan, stirring constantly over a low heat. Add the cocoa powder and a generous pinch of salt and continue to stir until everything has dissolved and blended.

5 Let the ganache cool enough not to melt the chocolate shells, but before it is solid, pour it into a plastic food bag. Snip off the tip of 1 corner to make a little hole and pipe ganache into each egg through the hole in the bag. Fill to just below the hole at the base of each egg.

6 Melt the remaining chocolate. Spoon some into each egg over the ganache to seal the chocolate shell. Wipe off any excess chocolate using a clean, damp cloth. Refrigerate until the chocolate has set. These will keep in the fridge for up to 2 weeks.

note *You could leave the eggs plain or decorate the shells. Print messages directly onto the shells using rubber stamps, or write or draw on them using metallic permanent pens.*

HALLOWEEN PARTY

We always have a Halloween party. The girls love it, and I love it, too – not just because it's fun and makes the kids happy! For selfish reasons, too – a Halloween party is the easiest one to throw, because most of it takes care of itself. Going around the local streets, filling up bags with free sweets from kind neighbours is, to children, one of the best things in the world. All you need to do is chaperone for 45 minutes or so.

Throw in a simple supper, some apple bobbing, scary statues (musical statues, but the children have to stop in a scary pose), witch's footsteps (like Grandma's footsteps but with a witch instead) and you've got a party. The party preparations can be almost as much fun for children as the event itself, and creating a few Halloween decorations together will really set the scene for some spooky fun.

halloween pumpkins

You can't have Halloween without pumpkins – the more, the better. On the business of how to pimp yours, there's a trend for producing mini artworks by sculpting designs onto the surface with a craft knife. These look amazing. But unless you've got so much time to spare you don't know what to do with it, the simplest way is still the crowd pleaser, in my book. Roughly carving out a crude face with the pointed tip of a sharp knife will take around 30 seconds. If you want something a bit more stylish, how about stars? They look fab, but require no artistic talent at all.

How to hollow out a pumpkin needs little explanation. The only thing I would say is that scooping out the insides is easiest with a teaspoon. Just keep scraping down the sides and tip everything out occasionally.

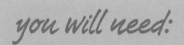 **you will need:**

- Pumpkin
- Star-shaped cookie cutter
- Hammer
- Battery operated tea lights

method

1 Cut out the stars before scraping out the pumpkin, using a cookie cutter and a hammer. Hammer the cookie cutter into the skin of the pumpkin to punch star shapes wherever you want them.

2 When you've done as many stars as you want, cut off the top of the pumpkin (keep it to use as a lid for your lantern) and get the kids to scrape the pumpkin clean.

3 Press out the cut stars, if they haven't fallen out already.

4 Place a battery operated tea light inside the pumpkin. (These offer a safe option for lighting up the pumpkin, and you can leave them on with the pumpkin lid on top to make a glowing globe.)

note *I love using miniature pumpkins simply hollowed out and with a tea light inside. Mix them up with traditional carved big pumpkins for maximum impact.*

floating ghosts

For a really effective spook-tacle, make these crazy floating ghosts!

method

1 Blow up the balloons.

2 Use a pencil to poke a small hole in the centre of each fabric square. To make a ghost, push the knotted bit of a balloon through the hole. Cut a length of clear thread that's long enough to hang up the ghost and tie this around the knot on the balloon.

3 To make the faces, cut out eye and mouth shapes (as shown in the picture opposite) from black fabric. Stick these onto the muslin over the balloon in the appropriate places using glue. Hang up the ghosts using the clear thread.

balloon lanterns

Pretty, glowing balloon lanterns are a stylish alternative to the floating ghosts above – or you could have both!

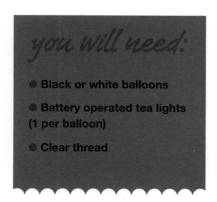
method

1 You can put these together as early as you like before the party, but leave them turned off inside the balloons until you are ready to hang the lanterns (which should be as late as possible before the party begins). Don't blow up the balloons at this stage – once they are blown up you won't be able to turn the tea lights on and off.

2 Stretch open the mouth of the balloon as much as you can so that you can squeeze the tea light into it. It's easiest for 1 person to stretch out the balloon while another pops a tea light inside.

3 When you're ready to hang up the lanterns, turn on the tea light inside by pressing the switch through the rubber balloon. Now blow up the balloons, knot them and hang them up using the clear thread.

bat bunting

This is one of those things that requires some effort when you make it, but on every subsequent occasion when you pull it out of a cupboard you'll have instant decorative style that's as pleasing as ever. Make light work of the bat cut outs by getting the children to pile in and help you.

you will need:

- Card
- White fabric pencil
- Black fabric (enough for 14 bats)
- 6m black cotton tape

method

1 Draw a bat shape like the one below on the piece of card and cut out. To make your bat symmetrical, fold the card in half and draw half a bat up to the fold so that when you cut it out both sides match.

2 Use the white fabric pencil to trace around the template onto the black fabric. You will need around 14 bats for 6 metres of cotton tape. Use sharp fabric scissors to cut out your bats.

3 The quickest and easiest way to sew the bats onto the tape is to machine-stitch in 1 continuous line through each wing. (If you sew them on by hand, use a few stitches to fix each wing to the tape.) Don't worry about spacing the bats perfectly or positioning them identically. Just place the bats as you go and sew.

note *Finish off your spooky decorations by hanging up a foraged branch painted black, draped with spider webs, spiders and bats.*

amazing goo

This goo is guaranteed to delight any kid, especially if they play a part in making it. I say delight the kids but, actually, I could play with this all day. Basically put some of the goo in your hand: if you keep your hand still, the goo runs like a liquid; scrunch up your hand and it hardens to form a solid shape. You can roll it into a ball, then relax your hand again and it goes gloopy. All you need to make it is some cornflour and water. Could anything be more cheap and cheerful?

you will need:

- ● **65g cornflour** (per person)
- ● **50ml water** (per person)
- ● **Glitter and food colouring** (optional)

method

1 Put the cornflour in a mixing cup or bowl. Add as much glitter as you like, if you're using any.

2 Add a few drops of food colouring, if you're using any, to the water.

3 Pour the water onto the cornflour and stir. It will be difficult to stir the mixture as it stiffens when it is moved, so once you've mixed as much as you can, leave it to sit, and it will just spread and mix on its own.

note *If you're making goo with a bunch of kids as a party activity, the easiest way is to give each child a resealable plastic bag for mixing, containing the cornflour. Let them add the glitter and pour in the coloured water. The goo can go back in the bag and be sealed shut to take home after the party. If the goo dries out a bit in the bag and becomes too stiff, add a little extra water to give it the right consistency. How's that for no-hassle, crowd-pleasing party bags?*

christmas glitter lanterns

Super spangly, this holiday decoration stays on just the right side of gaudy. The way the light reflects off the glitter lining of the jar is just so twinkly and pretty. It's very easy and practically free to make – it's just a glammed-up recycled jar. Put a bunch of these together on a table or shelf, or hang them from a hallway banister, or from the tree. If you hang them on the tree, use battery operated tea lights inside them for safety.

you will need:

- Clean jam jars
- Craft glue that dries clear
- Glitter
- 50cm length of wire or string (optional)
- Tea lights or battery operated tea lights

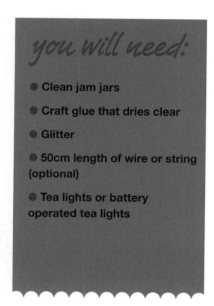

method

1 Splodge glue inside the jar with a paintbrush and spread it around the inside of the jar so it is completely covered with a fairly thin layer of glue. Work quite quickly, because you want to put in the glitter before the glue has started to dry.

2 Pour a generous amount of glitter into the jar and roll it around so that the glitter spreads and covers all of the gluey surfaces. Once the inside is completely covered, pour out the excess glitter onto a piece of paper, then roll up the paper in a cone shape so you can use it as a funnel through which to pour the glitter back into the glitter pot, so you can use it for another project.

3 If you are going to hang up your lantern, you will need to make a hanging loop. Wrap the string or wire around the neck of the jar and either tie or twist it tightly to secure it to the jar, leaving 1 short end and 1 very long end.

4 Pull the long loose end up over the jar to make a loop. Push it under the string or wire on the opposite side (use a knife to help you push it under) and knot or twist tightly. If you are hanging the lantern on a banister, you will need to tie this loop as you hang it.

5 Add a tea light. Gorgeous!

simple christmas cards

It's lovely to receive a homemade Christmas card, and making your own festive cards is a fun thing to do. Photographs are most commonly put on the front, but this is a really fabulous and fun alternative, which outsources all the work to the kids. And actually, it's no work for them, just fun – drawing a great picture, then doing loads of colouring in.

you will need:

● A4 paper

● Fine- or medium-tipped black permanent marker

● A4 art card

● Access to a photocopier

● Coloured pens/paint/glitter

method

1 Fold a sheet of A4 paper in half to make a card shape. Get your child to draw/doodle/write messages on the front half of the card using a fine-tipped black marker pen. Each child in your family could make their own design, or you could go for a collaborative montage and get everyone in the family to add their own little touch.

2 Photocopy the design onto A4 art card, ensuring that it is positioned so that the design appears on the front of the Christmas card when the A4 card is folded.

3 Now get your child to colour in their design, adding glitter to give it a festive touch if they like.

4 Fold the card in half as you did the A4 paper.

alternative *Use coloured or metallic card and leave the design in plain black, which looks simple and stylish.*

tip *These can be made any time of year, whenever the kids are agitating for something to do... like in the long summer holidays. It'll keep them entertained and get a job ticked off the Christmas to do list. Keep the pile of ready made cards stashed away, ready to pull out whenever they're bored!*

laced-up card

Inspired by Victorian folded letters that turned the written page into an envelope, this is just a very sweet but simple way of making a holiday thank you or sending new year wishes. Children love doing fiddly little things, so adding the twist of a lace tie to these missives might make the kids a little more keen to crack on with their post-Christmas thank yous. With most notes being sent by email these days, this is a lovely thing to receive in the post.

you will need:

- **Sheet of A4 paper**
- **Star punch or hole punch**
- **70cm-long torn fabric strip, ribbon or string**

method

1 Write, draw, stick on pictures, or do whatever you want on 1 side of the paper, avoiding the areas near the longer edges of the paper.

2 With the longer edges to the sides, fold down the top third of the paper, then fold again.

3 Punch 3 or 4 stars or holes evenly down the sides (which are now the shorter edges).

4 Fold the 2 side edges (the edges with the shapes cut out of them) towards the centre of the rectangle to meet in the middle.

5 Thread the ribbon, fabric strip or string through the holes as if you were lacing a shoe. Secure at the top or bottom with a bow.

6 Stamp and address the other side and post.

PRESENTS FOR KIDS TO MAKE FOR GROWN-UPS

...perfect for dads, grandpas, godfathers, uncles, teachers...

button cufflinks

Men are always losing their cufflinks, so this cute little pair will make a welcome and useful gift. If you use buttons from your stash, the cufflinks won't cost anything to make but do look really cool, making a virtue of the simplicity of a button. I am a sucker for pretty mother-of-pearl buttons, but you can use any buttons that take your fancy.

you will need:

● **Shirring elastic in bright colour (Gutermann has a good colour range)**

● **4 buttons, each with 4 holes (ensure they fit through cuff-sized buttonholes)**

method

1 Cut 2 x 20cm lengths of the shirring elastic. Take 1 of these and feed it diagonally through 2 holes in 1 of the buttons. Feed the second piece of elastic through the other 2 holes, so that the elastics are criss-crossed over the button.

2 Ensure the 4 pieces of elastic dangling beneath the button are all the same length. Combine them into 2 lots of 2, then knot the 2 lengths together. Now continue to knot the 2 lengths together until you have a 1cm-long 'chain', with the 4 free ends dangling from the end of the chain.

3 Feed the 4 ends of elastic separately through each hole of another button via the back of the button. Thread each end back through the diagonally opposite hole so the threads make a cross shape on the button.

4 Knot the threads tightly at the back of the button using a double knot. Cut the loose ends away, leaving 2mm of threads. The next part should be done by an adult. Very carefully light the loose ends with a match and let them burn for just a second so that the synthetic threads melt and meld together.

5 Repeat with the remaining 2 buttons to make a pair of cufflinks.

wood off-cut picture frame

A picture frame is always a great thing to give, especially if it contains a picture of the child who made it, or one drawn by them. The beauty of this frame is its simplicity, and it is guaranteed to have heart-squeezing pride of place on any desk.

A glazier will resize an offcut piece of glass for pennies.

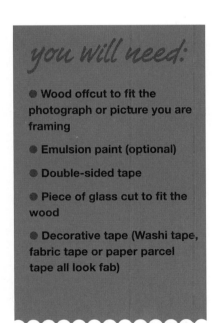

you will need:

● **Wood offcut to fit the photograph or picture you are framing**

● **Emulsion paint (optional)**

● **Double-sided tape**

● **Piece of glass cut to fit the wood**

● **Decorative tape (Washi tape, fabric tape or paper parcel tape all look fab)**

method

1 Putting this frame together takes no time at all. At its simplest, just leave the wood as it is. If you like, you can give the wood a wash of colour. Water down some emulsion paint, working with a ratio of 1 part water to 1 part paint. Apply it to the wood with a damp cloth. Leave to dry.

2 Fix the picture onto the wood with double-sided tape.

3 Align the glass with the wood over the picture. Stick decorative tape all the way around the edges of the glass so that it overlaps the glass and wood, to hold it all together. If the tape isn't wide enough, overlap with a second layer of tape.

note *If the frame is made by a really little child, it's cute to get them to 'sign' the back of the frame with a little painted handprint. If the child is older, they could write a message to the recipient of the gift with a permanent pen.*

shirt-and-tie card

This brilliant card was designed by one of the teachers at my youngest daughter's nursery. I just had to ask her if I could share it, so thank you, Miss Naheed, for saying yes! It is one of those lovely things that is deceptively simple, so can be made by very young children.

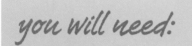

you will need:

- Paper
- Paints
- Sheet of A4-sized card

method

1 The tie is made from a child's artwork, so give the kids some paper and paint and leave them to it. Leave to dry.

2 Fold the A4 card in half to make a card shape. Cut a vertical 6cm-long slit halfway along the top of the card. Fold down 2 triangles of card on either side of the cut to create the shirt collar.

3 Cut out a tie shape from the painted paper. Using the picture opposite as a guide, glue it into position. Leave to dry. So simple, but so effective!

note *For a more grown-up version, cover the front of the card and the turned-down collar with fabric to make a shirt, and then cut out a fabric tie. You could go ultra psychedelic with clashing prints for a really funky look.*

daddy wallet

A handy credit card pouch, perfect for daddies...
but not exclusively so!

you will need:

● Good-quality 1mm-thick
wool felt measuring 21 x 8.5cm

● 2 pieces of fabric measuring
7 x 10cm

● 2 pieces of fabric measuring
5 x 10cm

method

1 Fold the felt in half widthways. Cut a little V-shaped nick across the fold at the top and bottom.

2 Place the 7 x 10cm pieces of fabric on the felt on the inside of the wallet either side of the nicks, using the picture opposite to guide you on their positions. Pin and sew around the sides and bottom of each piece of fabric, working as close to the edges of the fabric as possible (less than 5mm).

3 Position a 5 x 10cm piece of fabric on top of each of the stitched pieces, aligning the bottom and side edges and pin in place. Sew around the side edges and bottom as before. Couldn't be simpler.

note *This could be sewn by hand but, as usual, if you can use a sewing machine it is much quicker and easier. Use thread the same colour as the felt, so you won't see the stitches on the outside of the wallet.*

HOW-TO:

book corner

I came across the idea of a simple origami book corner when my daughter came home one day with one folded from a piece of paper torn out of her maths book. That book corner instantly pressed my magic buttons (it is simple and practical), so I came up with a pretty version to turn it into an ultra-useful gift for anyone, from teachers to grandparents. It's nice to give several of these, made using a variety of pretty fabrics.

you will need:

- 10cm square sheet of paper
- Spray craft glue
- 2 x 10cm square pieces of fabrics (either different fabrics or the same)

method

1 Put your piece of paper on a sheet of newspaper to protect your work surface. Cover it with the spray glue. Place 1 of the pieces of fabric on top and stick it down firmly, smoothing out any creases. Turn over the paper and repeat with the second piece of fabric. There's no need to allow the glue to dry before folding.

2 Turn the square so that it is a diamond shape. Fold the diamond in half, top to bottom, to turn it into a triangle and press the crease. If you have used 2 different fabrics, ensure the one you like best is on the outside of this folded triangle.

3 With the flat side of the triangle at the top, fold the 2 side points of the triangle down to meet the third point and press the crease. It will change the shape into a diamond.

4 Open out the folded triangular flaps. Now fold up the bottom half of the diamond; there are 2 layers – just fold the top layer for now, turning it into a triangle.

5 Now fold the triangular flaps back down over this section. Fold them in half and tuck the bottom half of each inside the book corner. You will now have a folded triangle on top, but the back layer will still be diamond shaped.

6 Fold the remaining diamond in half into a triangle. Tuck the bottom half of this triangle up inside the book corner.

note *Fow a how to video for this project, go to joannagosling.com*

...perfect for mums, grannies, godmothers, aunts, teachers...

lantern with knitted cover

One of my daughters made one of these for me from a small, unused rectangle of knitting I had left lying around – and I just love it! I make so many different types of tea light holders, but this is something I had never thought of doing before. The candle light looks so pretty twinkling through the loose knitted stitches. It's a simple knit, so perfect for a beginner, but for a younger child, this could be a collaborative project, with the child stitching together a rectangle knitted by someone else.

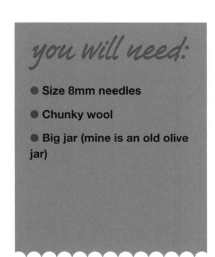

you will need:

- Size 8mm needles
- Chunky wool
- Big jar (mine is an old olive jar)

method

1 Cast on 15 stitches, leaving a long tail. Knit 40 rows. Cast off, leaving a long tail.

2 Use a loose end to stitch the short edges of the knitted piece together to make a tube.

3 Finish off the ends by tying them together in a bow.

4 Slip the cover over the jar.

note *To give this as a gift you could fill up the jar with tea lights and package it up with a fabric-covered box of matches.*

knitted lavender heart

A homemade knitted heart looks quite impressive but, actually, we're right back to the 'minimum effort, maximum return' mantra. With a simple trick, you can turn two basic knitted squares into one gorgeous heart.

you will need:

- ● Size 6.5mm needles
- ● Chunky wool
- ● 2 x 12cm square fabric squares
- ● Sheet of paper
- ● Dried lavender

method

1 Cast on 16 stitches. Knit 26 rows and cast off. Repeat to make a second square of the same size.

2 Align the 2 knitted squares. Align the fabric squares on the outside of the knitted squares. Pin the whole lot together.

3 Draw a heart which is slightly smaller than the fabric squares on some paper and cut it out to make a template. Pin it onto the fabric squares, pinning through all the layers (you can hold the layers together with clothes pegs if it's too bulky for pins).

4 Sew around the outside of the heart template, starting from the point of the heart at the bottom. Sew almost all the way around, stopping 5cm before the end.

5 Remove the paper heart. Turn the project the right way out so that the knitted layers are on the outside and it is heart-shaped.

6 Fill the heart with dried lavender.

7 Sew the gap closed.

8 Finger knit a 40cm length (see page 12). Fold it in half and tie the loose ends in a bow. Sew the hanging loop onto the dip of the heart, stitching through the bow to secure it.

Iona's safety pin bracelet

This was a gift from my daughter Iona, who is really good at spotting new uses for old things. She came up with this one day when she was using safety pins. I include it here as it's a perfect example of how unleashing a child's creativity allows them to see beauty in the most mundane of objects. And it's so easy to do, it's perfect for a little one to put together for Mother's Day.

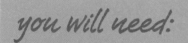

- **Approximately 8–10 safety pins (the number required depends on the size of the pins)**

method

Simply clip the safety pins together by putting the point of 1 through the gap of the next. Don't pass the point through the coiled hole at the end of the pin as, if you do, the bracelet won't lie flat. Repeat until you have the length you want.

note *You can jazz up the pins by threading beads, sequins, little bells, charms, shells or anything you like onto them. You might want to stick to silver-coloured accessories, or you could go really bright and colourful. Ensure you leave at least 1 pin with no embellishments, so that it can be used as the fastener without any threaded additions falling off.*

peppermint sugar foot scrub

Anything that offers the opportunity for a bit of relaxation is always a welcome gift, so here's an easy little thing to make for Mum that should be a big hit.

you will need:

- 400g golden caster sugar
- 250ml almond oil
- 10ml peppermint oil
- 5ml eucalyptus oil
- 10ml lime oil
- Large jar with lid
- Small square or rectangle of thin card
- Hole punch
- Long, thin strip of pretty fabric

method

1 Combine the sugar and the oils in a bowl. Transfer the mixture to a jar and put on the lid.

2 Punch a hole in the centre of one edge of the card square or rectangle using a hole punch. Write your message on this label. Now pass 1 end of the strip of fabric through the hole and centre the label along the strip. Tie the fabric strip around the neck of the jar and finish off with a pretty bow.

note *Perhaps give this gift with a nail varnish, too, and offer a spa-style pedicure!*

flower-imprinted clay block

This pretty imprinted block will last far longer than real flowers. The idea for it came one day when I was making something with air dry clay and my daughter came in from the garden with some daisies from the lawn. As they wouldn't last long in water, I thought I'd have a go at printing with them. This is a really lovely way to preserve a fleeting moment forever – every time I look at those pressed daisies I remember my joyous little three-year-old stumbling through the door with her booty clenched proudly in her hot little hand.

you will need:

- **Flowers**
- **Air dry clay**
- **Rolling pin**

method

1 First, gather your flowers in the garden or out on a walk. Even the smallest flowers will do. You could pick several of the same type or mix them up – whatever you like best.

2 Roll out the clay using a rolling pin. It should be about 3mm thick.

3 The shape you make the clay is entirely up to you. You can roll it out into a rough circle and leave it like that. Or cut away the sides and turn it into a square or rectangle. Or use a cookie cutter to make a heart or any other shape you like. You can put several flowers onto 1 piece, or cut out several pieces, each to be printed with 1 flower.

4 Lay the flower onto the clay where you want it with the front of the flower facing the clay or in profile, as in the photo, and press it in lightly with your fingers. Use the rolling pin to go over the flower and press it all the way into the clay. Carefully peel the flower out of the clay (it's easiest to start with the stalk). If you need to, use a pin to help lift the flower out of the clay or to pick out any delicate petals that are left behind. Leave to dry.

note *The dried clay block can be given just as it is or framed. It makes a lovely wedding gift, too. A friend who saw these in my house made a version for her best friend using the flowers in her wedding bouquet. I love that.*

fabric-and-glitter card

Making one of these cards takes only minutes, and it's so pretty, I love to give them for all occasions. I make variations of this card for kids and grown-ups alike. Because it's so simple to make, it's a great project for a child of any age.

you will need:

- A4 sheet of 200–300gsm art card
- Spray craft glue
- Piece of fabric that's a little larger than the card
- Heart-shaped cookie cutter (or use any other shape you like)
- Craft glue
- Glitter

method

1 Spray 1 side of the card with the spray glue. Immediately place the fabric onto it. I don't bother to cut fabric to size first. Simply place the fabric (which is larger than the card) onto the sticky card. Press it flat to ensure there are no wrinkles. Use scissors to cut the fabric to the same size as the card. Fold it in half.

2 Place the cookie cutter on the front of the card where you want your glittery shape to be. Hold it in position and brush craft glue into the shape, making sure you get the glue into any corners.

3 Remove the cookie cutter and pour glitter onto the wet glue. Tip away the excess glitter. Leave to dry.

note *You can simply write inside or, for a more fancy finish, print a greeting with rubber stamps. If you don't want a glitter design, you can paint within the shape of the cookie cutter instead.*

doggie birthday biscuits

I came up with a recipe for dog biscuits because the girls love to give our puppy special treats and they love to bake, so it seemed like a good idea to bring the two things together. The first time we made them we didn't use salmon oil. The girls loved them; the dog, not so much. With the added salmon oil, the dog loves them but the girls, not so much – as it should be!

Using cup measurements keeps this recipe ultra simple, as it means the kids don't have to weigh out the ingredients. Measuring cups can be bought cheaply and easily online. The measurements might vary slightly in different countries, but it doesn't matter, because the ratios of ingredients will still be correct.

you will need:

- 1 cup plain flour
- 1 cup oats
- 1 cup smooth peanut butter
- 25ml salmon or cod liver oil
- 3 eggs
- Rolling pin
- Cookie cutter

method

1 Preheat the oven to 200°C (gas 6).

2 Combine all the ingredients in a bowl and mix well using a fork and your hands. It will make a lovely, oily, almost rubbery – but not sticky – dough.

3 Sprinkle some flour onto the work surface and onto a rolling pin. Take a fistful of dough and roll it out so that it is about 2mm thick. Even though the dough is oily, it will flake apart a little as you roll it out. Just press any cracks together with your hands.

4 Use a small cookie cutter to cut out shapes from the rolled-out dough. If you don't have small cookie cutters, cut the dough into 2 x 2cm squares. Transfer to a baking tray lined with baking paper. The biscuits won't spread as they cook, so you don't need to leave big spaces between them.

5 Bake for 10 minutes. Leave to cool. They will keep for several weeks in an airtight jar.

for
KIDS

blackboard play table

This fantastic play table looks really cool and is just the right height for kids to sit around and play games, do puzzles, create and draw. The blackboard paint finish looks stylish and provides a surface on which the kids can draw pictures, practise letters and numbers, or play games. Because it's on wheels, it can be moved around easily. And the main part is free – a reclaimed pallet. Pick one up from a building site, or you may spot one abandoned on a street corner.

you will need:

- Pallet
- 4 large, chunky lockable castors
- Drill
- 16 screws
- Sheet of 15mm-thick MDF cut to fit the top of the pallet
- 4 nails
- Coloured paint
- Blackboard paint
- Paintbrush and roller

method

1 First, ensure the pallet is completely dry (it may have been outside for a while). If it is damp, stand it on one side for a day or two to allow it to dry out. If it's dirty, vacuum it to remove dust and dirt.

2 Position each castor on the underside of the pallet and make pencil marks on the wood through the 4 screw holes on each castor base plate. Use a small drill bit to make holes for the screws in the wood. Put the castors in place and screw them on.

3 Turn the table so that the right side is facing up. Place the MDF on top. Drill a small hole through each corner of the MDF into the pallet using a 2mm drill bit. Fix it onto the pallet by hammering a nail into each hole. Now the play table just needs a lick of paint.

4 Paint the pallet base – just the sides and inner parts that you can see. It's easiest to paint the rough wood with a wide, generously loaded paintbrush. Paint the edges of the MDF in the same colour.

5 Finally, paint the top of the MDF using blackboard paint. Use a roller for this. You'll need a few coats of blackboard paint. Sand it lightly in between coats to get a good, smooth finish.

note *There's plenty of storage space on the lower layer of slats for art supplies, toys, games, Lego and anything else you want to hide away, but have accessible.*

roll-away play board

When a major masterpiece of Lego construction or an intricate jigsaw is in progress, this play board acts as a moveable bit of floor that allows you to shift the work-in-progress out of the way when the kids are finished for the day. When the work is complete, the play board can be stored standing on its side so that it takes up minimum space. And it couldn't be simpler to make. Size it according to the space you have and what the kids intend to use it for and this will be one of those 'why didn't I think of that before?!' projects.

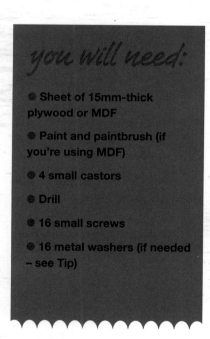

you will need:

● Sheet of 15mm-thick plywood or MDF

● Paint and paintbrush (if you're using MDF)

● 4 small castors

● Drill

● 16 small screws

● 16 metal washers (if needed – see Tip)

method

1 If you're using plywood, you can just leave it as it is, unpainted. If you're using MDF, you'll need to paint it. So prop up the board on blocks to paint the top and sides. Give it as many coats as you need to get a good finish. When the top is dry, flip it over to paint the underside. Normally, I wouldn't bother to paint the underside of anything – why bother if it won't be seen? In this case, however, if you are going to be standing it on its side when not in use, the base will be visible.

2 To fix on the castors, use a pencil to mark drill points onto the wood through the screw holes in the castor base plates. To ensure you don't drill all the way through to the top of the board, hold the drill bit up against the side of the board to gauge how deeply you need to drill, then place a piece of masking tape on the drill bit to mark the depth of the hole you need to drill, as a guide. Ensure you use short screws that won't go all the way through the wood. Drill small holes into the plywood or MDF for the screws. Position the castors and screw them on.

tip *If the heads of the small screws are too small for the castors, put metal washers between each screw and castor, to hold the castor in place.*

note *You can glue things onto the play board, such as Lego base plates or train tracks, to give it a dedicated use.*

104

rolling storage boxes

Four simple wheels screwed on the bottom of a box instantly make it a brilliantly practical storage option. You or the kids can wheel it to wherever you want it (no heavy lifting or scraping the floor!), and it can just as easily be pushed away when playtime's over. I've used one of my favourite upcycling basics for this project – an old wooden wine crate. I paint mine with blackboard paint and scrawl the contents of the box on the side with chalk. Make a few of these and you have a series of mini dump zones for things like Lego, musical instruments, role-play toys, craft supplies, shoes and so on. And, come tidy-up time, everyone knows exactly what goes where.

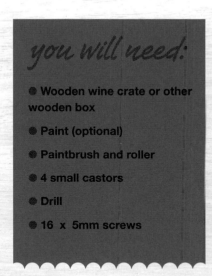

you will need:

- Wooden wine crate or other wooden box
- Paint (optional)
- Paintbrush and roller
- 4 small castors
- Drill
- 16 x 5mm screws

method

1 Prop up the box on blocks and paint it. Use a roller for speed and the best finish, and a brush to infill any areas the roller won't reach.

2 Once the paint is dry, position each castor on the underside of the box and make pencil marks on the wood through the 4 screw holes on each castor base plate. Use a small drill bit to make holes for the screws in the wood. Put the castors in place and screw them on.

note *These boxes also look fabulous with numbers, words or shapes printed on the side using stencils. Simply tape the stencil onto the side of the box and lightly sponge paint onto it. You can make a simple stencil from a piece of card. To make letter or number stencils, choose a font you like on a computer and scale it up to the size you want, then print it out and transfer it onto card. To do this, rub pencil over the back of the printed paper. Place it on top of the cardboard, then trace over the shape with the point of a pencil. Now use a craft knife to cut out the stencil.*

fruit crate wardrobe

These easy access compartments offer a much better storage solution for children than a hanging space that's too high for them to reach. And it's an efficient use of space, too, as you can get so much into the boxes. Measure your space to establish how many boxes you'll need. Providing your wall is sound, these are easy to put up. Here's how…

You can either hunt out fruit crates at markets or – much easier – type 'fruit crate' into an online search engine, which should throw up a plethora of suppliers. If you can't get hold of them, any wooden boxes will do, but try to source boxes with similar dimensions to those of fruit crates (55 x 37 x 35cm), which allow for plenty of storage.

you will need:

● Fruit crates (or similar-sized boxes)

● 4 screws per box

● Spirit level

● Drill

● 4 universal rawl plugs per box

● Round hooks (optional)

method

1 Establish the position for the bottom row. Consider leaving enough space underneath for hanging clothes. Start in the middle of the bottom row and work outwards on either side. Hold up the first crate where you want it to be on the wall. Place a spirit level on top of the box and, when you're satisfied with its position, draw a pencil line around the box. Write the number 1 on the crate and also inside the pencil outline on the wall. (This is just in case the size or shape of each box varies slightly.) Position the second box right next to the first and repeat. Continue until you have marked the positions for all the boxes in the bottom row.

3 Drill 4 screw holes into corners of the base (i.e. the side that will sit against the wall) of each crate. Hold up box number 1 and use a bradawl or pencil to mark the drill points on the wall through the holes. Drill holes into the wall and fix the rawl plugs. Screw the box onto the wall. Repeat with the remaining boxes in the bottom row.

4 The next row will be easier because you can sit the boxes on top of the first row rather than having to hold them up in position. Repeat the process until all your crates are on the wall.

5 If you want to hang some clothes below, attach round hooks to the underside of the bottom row of boxes. Start the hole with a bradawl, then screw in the hooks. You can put a line of several hooks on each box, one behind the other, depending on how much stuff you want to hang up.

note *The quickest and easiest way to cover the wardrobe is with a cheat's curtain – a length of fabric fixed on with drawing pins. You can pull them back out of the way by tucking them into the hand holes on the sides of the crates.*

trundle bed

Not many weekends go by without at least one extra child – and sometimes several – staying for a sleepover. These pull-out beds are just brilliant for accommodating extra bodies with zero hassle. Proper trundle beds can be very expensive, which seems crazy since they're not sprung like a proper bed – they're simply a base-board with sides. So here's the pared-down version. It does the job, but costs very little to make.

you will need:

- **Sheet of 3cm-thick MDF (the size depends on the bed – measure your space and ensure a mattress will fit)**
- **6 x 30mm castors**
- **Drill**
- **30 screws**
- **Paint**
- **Mattress**
- **Two small strips of fabric**

method

1 Position the castors on the underside of the MDF board – you'll need 1 at each corner and 2 in the middle. Make holes for the screws by drilling through each screw hole on the castor with a small drill bit first. Screw the castors onto the underside of the MDF.

2 Paint the top and sides of the MDF. Leave to dry, then put your mattress on top.

3 Choose where you want your handles to go, and then use a bradawl to make small holes for the screws. They need to be slighter closer together than the length of the pieces of fabric. Make small holes in the fabric for the screws to go through, and then screw them onto one side of the MDF.

note *Make sure your mattress will slide under the space beneath the bed. Trundle mattresses are not as deep as normal mattresses, so you may want to use one of these. Futon mattresses are a cheap option and look nice as they are finished in pretty fabric. If you're using a regular mattress, prettify it by covering it with fabric. Ensure the fabric is long enough to tuck underneath generously, so it stays put. If the fabric isn't wide enough for the mattress, use 2 lengths of fabric. Cut 1 in half lengthways and sew each of the halves onto either side of a full-width length.*

simple quilt

Beautiful fabric quilts look so pretty, but they are so expensive to buy. So, as usual, I had to come up with my own simple version using an old duvet, cheap and cheerful fabrics for the main body of the quilt and offcuts of a favourite Liberty print for a smart finish. Machine-washable style!

you will need:

- **Old single duvet (one with synthetic filling allows you to stick the whole thing in the washing machine and tumble dry or line dry easily)**

- **2 x 2.25m lengths of fabric for the main body of the duvet (use either different fabrics or the same for each side)**

- **6cm-wide torn strips of fabric for the edging (you'll need about 7m in all)**

method

1 First, cut out the rectangles of fabric for each side of the quilt. They need to be of the same dimensions as the duvet – 135 x 200cm is standard, but double check your duvet label.

2 Lay out 1 piece of fabric on the floor with the right side facing down. Align the duvet on top. Now align the second piece of fabric on top of the duvet, right side facing up. Pin it all together, then machine-stitch all the way around, about 1.5cm in from the edge.

3 Fold the fabric strips in half lengthways and pin them around the edges of the quilt with the fold over the edge. Stitch them on with the sewing machine, sewing about 2cm in from the raw edges of the fabric strips. Use a medium-length stitch setting. Don't worry about the raw edges – they look great and won't fray very much. Also, leaving them unhemmed keeps this project in the realms of 'minimum effort, maximum return'.

note *If the fabric you are using isn't wide enough, sew 2 lengths together to make a double width. Pin it onto the duvet with the seam running down the centre, then cut away any excess. Do this for both sides, then align the fabrics with the duvet as above and pin and sew the whole lot together.*

tip *Tear the 6cm-wide fabric strips for the edging from cotton fabric, which tears easily. Simply make a 2cm-long nick at the edge of the fabric and pull apart. It doesn't matter how long or short each strip is, so use up old scraps, mixing and matching fabrics, if you like.*

simple cushions

The Simple Quilt technique (see page 110) can be used to whizz up fabulous scatter cushions, too. You can use synthetic or feather cushion pads for this as both can easily be machine washed and tumble dried or line dried, as they are small.

you will need:

● Uncovered cushion pad

● 2 pieces of fabric, each slightly larger than the cushion (use either different fabrics or the same)

● 6cm-wide torn strips of fabric for the edging (you'll need about 3m in all)

method

1 Lay out 1 piece of fabric on the floor with the right side facing down. Align the cushion pad on top. Squish the air out of the cushion so that it is as flat as possible, then pin it to the fabric. Cut the fabric around the cushion pad. Cut a second piece of fabric to the same size.

2 Place the second piece of fabric on top of the cushion with the right side facing up. Machine-stitch around 1.5cm from the edges to sew the fabrics and cushion together.

3 Fold the edging fabric strips in half lengthways and pin them around the edges of the covered cushion with the fold over the edge. Machine-stitch these in place, sewing through the edges of the cushion pad, 2cm in from the edge.

fabric-covered magnetic board

This is great for an older child's bedroom. It's a pretty and neat way of displaying drawings and paintings, photographs, notes, reminders and anything else kids want on show or need to remember. And when they become bored of the fabric, it's easy to ring the changes – simply take the board off the wall and re-cover it.

An online search for 'magnetic steel cut to size' will throw up a range of suppliers.

you will need:

● **Sheet of magnetised steel, cut to the size you want; ask the metal cutter to punch a hole in each corner – or you can easily drill through it**

● **Drill**

● **4 x size 8 rawlplugs**

● **Piece of fabric slightly larger than the metal**

● **Sticky tape**

● **4 large screws**

method

1 Hold your metal sheet in position against the wall, ensuring it is straight. Poke a pencil through the holes at each corner to mark drill points on the wall. Drill 4 holes on your marks. Push a rawlplug into each hole.

2 Now cover the metal with your fabric. Fold it over the sides of the sheet and use sticky tape to stick it onto the back of the board to hold it in place. Cut little slits through the fabric where it has covered the holes in the metal in order to allow the screws to pass through the fabric.

3 Screw the board onto the wall. Now all your display board needs is a bunch of magnets, ready to hold an array of treasures.

shelf desk

This brilliant space saver is very easy to put up. It's simply an oversized shelf – all you need to do is fix it at the right height. It looks stylish and streamlined, and offers a practical work surface. And it's cheap to make as well. All boxes ticked… Ideally, you need three walls (although two will do) to provide an easy way in which to support the desk (so that you don't need to faff with special brackets), so this desk is perfect for an alcove.

you will need:

- 5cm x 2cm timber – the length must be enough to span the width and both sides of the desk

- Drill

- Spirit level

- 9 x size 8 rawlplugs

- 9 long screws

- Sheet of 5cm-thick MDF measuring 45cm x the width of the alcove

- 2 x 25mm L-shaped metal brackets

- Flexible filler

- Paint

method

1 First, cut a piece of the timber support to the same width as the desk. Drill 5 evenly spaced holes along its length into the 5cm span.

2 The height of the desk needs to be about 75cm, so you need to attach the timber support for the desktop onto the wall 70cm from the floor, as the desktop is 5cm thick. Hold up the timber support so that the top is 70cm from the floor. Balance the spirit level on the wood to ensure it is straight. Poke a pencil or bradawl through the holes you drilled into the wood to mark drill points on the wall.

3 Drill into the wall at the 5 points you have marked. Push a rawlplug into each hole. Reposition the timber and screw it onto the wall.

4 Now cut 2 shorter lengths to support the 2 sides of the desk. (If you only have 1 side wall, cut just 1 shorter length.)

5 Drill 2 holes through each support. Follow the instructions above to fix these onto the side walls.

6 Balance the MDF desktop on the timber frame. Fix the desktop securely onto the timber support with the L-shaped brackets. Screw one half of each bracket into the underside of the desk and the other into the timber batten. Two brackets along the width of the desk will suffice.

7 Use flexible filler to fill any gaps between the wall and MDF. If you have a particularly wide gap, pack it first with scrunched up paper, then cover over with filler using a filling knife. Once the filler has dried, paint the desk and timber supports.

i heart you picture

This makes a gorgeous feature in a child's room, but the added beauty is that a child can be involved with creating it. If they're little, use their scribblings and paint-splodged pictures to make the hearts. If they're bigger, make it en famille, sitting around, cutting out, sticking and gossiping as you go...

You could simply cut a large heart shape from something special and frame it for this project, but this über version looks as if it could hang in a gallery and doesn't require any more skill than the single, simple heart – just a bit more time.

you will need:

- Frame
- Fabric or paper to fill the inside of the frame (as a background)
- Double-sided tape
- Watered-down paint and a sponge
- A selection of things to cut the heart shapes out from: you could use your childrens' drawings, newspapers, wallpaper samples, photos – anything you like
- Glue stick

method

1 There is usually a paper insert inside the frame – remove this. You can use it to make the heart template for your design. If there isn't one, cut a piece of paper to size. Draw as large a heart as you want onto the paper. It doesn't matter if it's not perfect the first time. This paper is only going to be used as a guide for the heart, so keep reshaping it until you are happy. Use a craft knife to cut out the heart. Discard the heart-shaped cut-out – you'll use the paper from which it was cut as your stencil.

2 Next, cut a piece of paper or fabric to cover the board inside the frame and use double-sided tape to stick it onto the board.

3 Place your heart stencil onto the fabric or paper and dab watered-down paint onto the fabric or paper inside the cut-out heart shape using a damp sponge. Leave to dry.

4 Now cut out as many hearts as you will need to cover the painted heart. They can be all different sizes and absolutely do not have to be perfect – imperfection is the appealing hallmark of homemade. It's fun to sit around and cut these out with children as a team effort. The easiest way to cut heart shapes is to fold whatever you are cutting in half and cut half a heart against the fold. When you open it out, each half of the heart is a mirror image of the other.

5 Glue the cut-out hearts over the painted-on heart using a glue stick. If you've got a box frame, it's nice to stick some down completely but fold others in half, so they look as if they are fluttering off the page.

6 Put the fabric or paper in the frame. Your picture is now ready to hang.

hanging branch

Whenever we go out for a walk, the girls and I always come back with a haul of treasures – pine cones, shells, stones and sticks. Mostly, the sticks are put on the fire but, occasionally, we'll find one that's just too beautiful to destroy, so we have to keep it. This project offers a gorgeous way of breathing new life into an old, gnarled and stunning branch. You could hang this as a permanent fixture in a child's room, or put one up as a temporary decoration for a party or any other occasion.

you will need:

- **2 hook eyes**
- **String**
- **Branch or stick**
- **Toy birds, butterflies, stars, dinosaurs, planes, pompoms or any type of decoration you like**
- **Garden wire, clear thread, wool, tape or Blu Tack**

method

1 Fix the hook eyes into the ceiling to suspend the branch from, placing them about the length of the branch apart. Screwing into a ceiling may require a bit of trial and error, so I'm afraid this is the hardest part. Poke a bradawl into the spot at which you would like to fix a hook and make a small hole. Push the hook into it and screw it in. If you're lucky, it will get a good fix. If not, try again in a different spot. The worst that can happen is that you will end with a series of small error holes that can quickly be fixed with a blob of ready-made filler and a brush of paint. If you're not confident about the strength of your hooks, it's probably a good idea to hang up a light branch!

2 Tie the end of 1 piece of string onto 1 end of the branch, knotting it tightly so it won't slip or come undone. Hold up the branch at the height at which you want your branch to be suspended. Thread the string through one of the ceiling hooks and secure. Repeat at the other end.

3 Now decorate the branch with hanging pompoms, flowers, birds, butterflies, velociraptors, stars, planets or anything else you like. Fix your decorations onto the branch with garden wire, tape or Blu Tack, or suspend them using clear thread or colourful wool. Fairy lights twisted around the branch also look stunning.

bedside stash pocket

This is especially useful for bunk beds or in a bedroom where there's no space for a bedside table. It's a simple weighted pocket that slips over the edge of the bed, ready to stash a child's night-time must-haves, such as a book, a torch, a bottle of water... You could make one of these for the TV remote control, too.

you will need:

- 2 pieces of fabric measuring 25 x 45cm
- 1 piece of fabric measuring 21 x 32cm for the pocket
- 250g rice

method

1 Align the 2 larger pieces of fabric with the right sides facing in. Sew them together around 3 edges (2 long and 1 short), allowing a 5mm seam allowance.

2 Turn the sleeve so the right sides of the fabric are facing out. Firmly press the fabric with your hands so that the seams lie flat. (You could use an iron, but this is less faff.)

3 Now sew the pocket onto this sleeve. Centre the pocket 3cm above the base of the sleeve (the base is the sewed-up shorter edge). Sew around 3 sides (the 2 long sides and the base) to make an open pocket – don't worry about folding the edges of the pocket under.

4 To make the pouch for the rice (which acts as a weight), sew a row of stitches 5cm above the top of the open pocket. Now tuck the unfinished edges along the top of the sleeve inwards, folding the fabric over by about 1cm. Pin, then sew the edges together, leaving a 6cm opening at one end. Fill the pouch with rice.

5 Pin the opening of the rice pouch together, then stitch it closed.

tip *Make a funnel using a rolled-up piece of paper and stick one end of it into the rice pouch. Pour the rice through the funnel into the pouch to fill it.*

coat hanger dream catcher

Most children have bad dreams from time to time. It's comforting for children to talk through them, as together you work out the little snippet of a conversation, or the brief image in a movie, or barely noticed picture that hooked their unconscious mind in the daytime and allowed their imagination to go into overdrive in sleep, weaving a tale from the fragments. If a child keeps having bad dreams, these sweet dream catchers are a good thing to make together. Simple to do, pretty to look at and comforting for little ones.

you will need:

- Wire coat hanger
- Double-sided tape
- Torn strips of various fabrics
- String or ribbons
- Feathers
- 1 screw hook

method

1 First of all, stretch out the hanger and shape it into a circle. Stick a strip of double-sided tape around the tip of the hanging hook. Fix the end of a strip of fabric or ribbon around the tape, then twist the fabric around the metal repeatedly. When you come to the end of a strip, fix it to the wire with double-sided tape. Repeat until the entire circle is covered.

2 Now make the web. Tie the end of a strip of fabric or ribbon to the frame. Now criss-cross it across the frame, winding it around as you go to keep it in place. When you've criss-crossed it as many times as it will go, secure the end with a knot around the frame. Repeat with more strips of fabric to create a web effect.

3 Finally, tie several lengths of string to hang down from the bottom of the dream catcher. Tie feathers onto the string.

4 Fix a screw hook into the ceiling above the child's bed by making a small hole with a bradawl and screwing the hook into it. Hang up the dream catcher. Sweet dreams.

note *A dream catcher makes a great present for other children, especially if your own children help to make it. You could package it up with a copy of The BFG, the tale of the friendly dream-catching giant created by the legendary children's author Roald Dahl.*

jam jar night light

This cute little night light gives out just enough of a glow to provide comfort without disrupting sleep.

you will need:

● Old jar

● Star-shaped stickers (you can buy these very easily from any stationery store)

● Spray paint

● Battery operated tea light

method

1 First, ensure the jar is completely clean or the paint might not stick properly. To remove any sticky residue, either use a special sticky stuff remover, or try white spirit or nail varnish remover.

2 Remove the lid and dot the little star-shaped stickers all over the jar.

3 Lay out some newspaper and put something on it (like a block of wood – anything that you don't mind getting covered in paint) to stand your jar on for painting. Position the jar upside-down on the block. Spray paint the glass, building up an opaque covering with several thin coats, letting it dry between applications.

4 When the paint is completely dry, carefully peel away the stickers.

5 Put the jam jar upside-down over a battery operated tea light. Turn it on at bedtime.

bedside water jar

These pretty bedside carafes couldn't be less effort to make, but will save you from the familiar refrain after lights out of 'I'm thirsty!'

you will need:

● Recycled tall glass jar (the ones passata comes in are perfect)

● 1 temporary tattoo

method

1 Remove any labels from the jar and scrub it well.

2 Apply a temporary tattoo, just as you would onto skin. Fill the jar with water and place an upturned plastic cup or glass on top.

Note *The tattoo will survive careful hand washing, but you may need to replace it if it gets scruffy over time.*

hanging display

This simple hanging display takes minutes to put up, but it looks really cute and provides an incredibly useful way of keeping little mementoes and bits and pieces safe. Plus it uses very little space, as it holds objects vertically. It is also a very handy place to store hair clips so they're not forever disappearing into thin air.

you will need:

● **Length of 2cm-wide ribbon or torn fabric (the length required depends on ceiling height and how low you want it to hang)**

● **1 screw eye**

● **Something with a hole in it to act as a weight – a pebble or shell could work**

● **Wooden pegs**

● **Paint, fabric or pretty paper**

● **Double-sided tape**

method

1 Decide where you want to hang your display. Now make a small hole in the ceiling using a bradawl and screw the screw eye into it to fix it to the ceiling.

2 Tie the ribbon or fabric onto the metal loop of the screw eye and knot it tightly so that it won't come undone.

3 Tie the object you are using as a weight to the bottom of the ribbon or fabric.

4 You can use plain pegs to hang photographs, tickets and any other treasured items onto the ribbon or fabric, but if you prefer, paint the pegs, or cover them with fabric or paper. To cover them, stick double-sided tape onto the front and back of each peg, then fix the paper or fabric onto the tape and cut it to size.

spray-painted storage jars

There is not a single room in my house that doesn't have at least one old jam jar being used for something new. To reuse one for storage, you don't really have to do anything to it – wash it out, scrub off the old label, screw on the lid and it will do the trick. With a tiny bit of effort, though, you can turn an old jar into something that looks great and provides perfect storage for all the little bits and bobs that accumulate, such as hair clips, elastic bands, dice, beads, marbles, play dough or small bits of Lego, to name just a few.

I like to use white spray surface primer for these jars as I love the totally matt but ultra durable finish.

you will need:

● Old jars with lids
● Sticky backed plastic
● White spray surface primer

method

1 First, draw a shape – like a heart or a star – on sticky backed plastic to stick onto each jar. This will allow you to create a little window into the jar so that you can get a glimpse of what's inside.

2 Cut out the plastic shape, remove the backing and stick it onto the jars. Press it down firmly so that it sticks well, to ensure that paint won't leach under the edges.

3 Lay out some newspaper – it's a good idea to cover a large area, as droplets of spray paint can travel far. Prop up each jar (with the lid on) on a block and spray paint the outside. I love spray painting because it's super fast and you get a great finish. Ensure you don't spray too close, or you might end up with drips in the paint.

4 Once the paint is dry, peel off the sticky backed plastic and your jars are ready to use.

felt and finger-knitted bunting

A length of bunting made of felt shapes in pretty colours looks gorgeous in a child's bedroom and is very simple to create. It's a really nice little project to do with a child – the only skills required are finger knitting, cutting and simple sewing. This bunting makes a great gift, too.

Finger knitting is a great skill to teach your children – it's fun to do and is incredibly easy. In minutes you can make knitted lengths that can be turned into all sorts of things. See page 12 for instructions.

you will need:

● **Wool**

● **Felt – buy a mixed bag of small off-cuts in many colours (an online search will throw up plenty of options)**

● **Colourful tape**

method

1 Finger knit a length as long as you want your bunting to be (2–3m is a good length) or, better still, let your child do it.

2 Now cut out felt discs (or any shape you like). I used 2 coins in different sizes and a roll of tape for templates.

3 Once all the shapes are cut out, sew them onto the finger-knitted length. You or your child could do this by hand, but it will take some time. It's easier and quicker to use a sewing machine if you have one. Don't worry about spacing the felt shapes perfectly evenly. Simply position and sew as you go, working a continuous run of stitches from start to finish. Mix up the colours randomly. If you've cut the felt shapes to different sizes, mix those up, too.

4 Stick the bunting onto the wall using colourful tape.

tape measure height chart

Kids love to see how much they've grown, and height charts have spawned quite an industry. I've always preferred the old-fashioned way my parents charted our growth – by marking points on a door frame and scribbling our names next to them. I still love to see the marks every time I open their hallway cupboard, and I remember clearly standing inside the frame, excitedly waiting to find out if I had grown. My (slightly posher) version of the same is to stick a measuring tape to the doorframe. Actually, I stuck two onto ours as I understand feet and inches better, whereas the children work in centimetres.

you will need:

- 1 or 2 fabric measuring tapes
- Double-sided tape

method

1 Simply run double-sided tape along the length of the tape(s) on the back. Peel off the backing and fix the tape(s) to the doorframe. If you are using 2 tapes, fix them side by side so that you can tell at a glance the height measured in both metric and imperial units of measurement.

2 Either use a pen to write the child's name and the date next to their height each time you measure, or you can print out the details on a label maker, if you have one, to stick to the doorframe at the correct height to make it look super smart.

printers' tray model display

Old printers' trays make great display frames for collections of the little objects children love to hoard – Lego figures, collectible figurines, tin soldiers, animals, fossils… Whatever the latest craze, lining up the small treasures in the perfectly sized little wooden windows is a neat and attractive way of storing them. You might even fall slightly in love with the clutter when it looks so good!

Old printers' trays can be picked up fairly cheaply at markets or online. You can, of course, leave them as they are, in a natural wood finish, but they can be transformed with a coat of ultra bright paint for a really hip splash of colour in a kid's room.

you will need:

- ● **Printers' tray**
- ● **Spray paint (optional)**
- ● **Drill**
- ● **Spirit level**
- ● **2 universal rawlplugs**
- ● **2 screws**

method

1 If you're going to paint the tray, give it a good scrub with a toothbrush, bicarbonate of soda and soapy water first, as they can be quite grimy, which might make the paint peel. Leave the wood to dry completely before painting.

2 The easiest way to paint it is to use spray paint, as the little cubby holes make for a very fiddly job with a brush. Build up thinnish layers, to avoid drips, letting the paint dry between coats.

3 To hang it on a wall, drill a screw hole into a cubby hole on both the left and right sides of the tray, about halfway up. Position the tray on the wall. Balance a spirit level on top to ensure it is straight, then mark the drill points on the wall through the screw holes with a pencil or bradawl.

4 Drill holes into the wall and push universal rawlplugs into them. Fix the screws through the tray. It's a good idea to hang the display frame fairly low, or else above a sofa or chair so the kids can reach their toys.

starry starry night wall

You can liven up a plain painted wall with a cute and simple touch using homemade cork stamps. Perhaps get the kids involved in drawing shapes on corks saved from wine bottles, which you can then cut out for them.

These cork stamps can be used for anything. Use them to breathe new life into a plain T-shirt with little stars, decorate plain paper to make pretty wrapping, or dot stamped patterns all over a plain card. A homemade cork stamp is a small thing that keeps on giving.

you will need:

- An old cork from a bottle of fizz
- Craft knife
- Paint

method

1 Draw a star onto the flat end of the cork. Cut away the excess cork around the shape using a craft knife. Cut away to a depth of 5mm so that the stamper has a clean outline.

2 Now simply cover the star with a thin coat of paint and stamp away. Make sure the whole shape is printed by evenly pressing each point of the star as you go.

star cushions

I love making cushions, one of the simplest, most practical and pleasing makes if you've got a spare twenty minutes. In a flash you can come up with something that changes the feel of a room. They can add a splash of colour and, piled high, a feeling of lived-in homeliness and comfort. As you might have realised by now, I love star shapes, and I reckon this combination of comfort and design is pretty perfect for a child's bedroom.

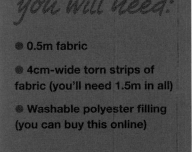

you will need:

- 0.5m fabric
- 4cm-wide torn strips of fabric (you'll need 1.5m in all)
- Washable polyester filling (you can buy this online)

method

1 Create a star template by drawing a five-pointed star on a 25cm square piece of paper or card and cutting it out.

2 Fold your large piece of fabric in half widthways and pin the template on top. This way, you will make 2 star shapes at once. Cut out the shapes.

3 Align the fabric stars together with the right sides facing out. Now pin the torn fabric strips around the edges of the star, folding them in half over the raw edge as you go and overlapping any joins.

4 Machine-stitch around the edges of the star about 1.5cm away from the edge, leaving 1 point of the star unstitched.

5 Fill the cushion with stuffing, using a knitting needle or chopstick to push the filling into the tips of the star's points.

6 Sew up the unstitched point, leaving a small gap for filling it. Now fill this last point with stuffing, then sew it closed.

note *This cushion can go in the washing machine at 30°C if you need to wash it. Pull it back into shape before leaving it to dry.*

knitted patchwork blanket

A gorgeous, simple project, whose beauty and joy also come from the fact that it can be a family collaboration. It is made up of small knitted squares that are sewn together. It does require a lot of squares, but each one takes very little time to make. So even though it's a relatively big project, it's not overwhelming, because it is made in bite-sized chunks. And, of course, anyone can knit these, so why not enlist every knitter in the family to come up with contributions? That way, it will feel like a really special family heirloom, made with love, with and for those you love.

you will need:

- Size 8mm needles
- Chunky wool in your chosen colours
- Wool for sewing up
- Darning needle
- Felt, cut into star shapes (optional)

method

1 For each square, cast on 15 stitches. Knit 22 rows and cast off. This should give you a square measuring approximately 12 x 12cm.

2 For a baby blanket, knit 30 squares. Stitch them together with wool, in a block of 5 across and 6 down. This will make a blanket measuring approximately 60 x 72cm.

3 You could leave the blanket as it is, or sew on little felt stars, as I have done.

note *This blanket could be made larger for a bigger childs' bed but, obviously, that would be a longer project, which you may or may not be prepared to take on, depending on your patience. No one likes a project that outstays its welcome. You could make a small blanket and then gradually add more squares to it over time.*

knitted patchwork cushion

This pretty cushion makes a nice addition to the knitted patchwork blanket on page 140, or is a good alternative project that's quicker to make, since it requires fewer squares.

you will need:

- Size 8mm needles
- Chunky wool in your chosen colours
- Darning needle
- 50 x 50cm cushion pad
- Wool for finger knitting

method

1 Cast on 15 stitches. Knit 22 rows and cast off. This should give you a square measuring 12 x 12cm. Knit 18 squares.

2 Sew 9 of the squares together in 3 rows of 3. Repeat with the remaining 9 squares.

3 Align the 2 patchwork pieces with the right sides facing out. Sew them together around 3 edges, leaving 1 side open through which to insert a cushion pad.

4 Finger knit 6 x 20cm lengths (see page 12 for instructions on finger knitting). Take 1 of these lengths and weave the loose end at 1 end into the finger-knitted length to hide it. Use the other loose end to stitch it onto the opening of the cushion cover. Repeat with the other finger-knitted lengths. Sew 3 on each side of the opening – 1 in the middle and 2 at the edges of each side.

5 Insert the cushion pad, then close the cushion by tying the finger-knitted lengths in bows.

fabric-covered tooth fairy box

It can't be just my household in which the excitement of a fallen-out tooth is ruined when the child realises they've misplaced said tooth, can it? This little box is a safe place to stash teeth as soon as they come out. Plus, it's easier for the tooth fairy to pull out a box from under the pillow than to have to rummage around in the dark for a tiny tooth, worrying that the commotion might wake the child... or is that just my house again?

you will need:

- Empty matchbox
- Fabric scraps
- Double-sided tape

method

1 First, cover the inside of the pull-out tray of the box (the bit the matches go into). Using the base of the tray as a template, cut out a rectangle of fabric for the inside base. Cover the underside of the fabric with double-sided tape and stick the fabric onto the base of the tray.

2 Line the rest of the inside of the tray with small rectangles fixed with double-sided tape. Don't cover the outside of the tray – it will make it too thick to slide in and out of the slipcover.

3 Cover the slipcover with a piece of fabric that's cut to size, again, sticking it on with double-sided tape.

4 To decorate the box, stick a fabric cut-out shape onto the top of the box with double-sided tape. Alternatively, print a name or initials using rubber or homemade cork stamps (see page 138). Now you just need to pray that the tooth fairy doesn't forget...

simple skirt

I love to make these little skirts for my daughters. They can be rustled up so quickly and will be worn endlessly. You can keep your skirt really simple and do no more than sew the sides of a strip of fabric together, hem the top and bottom and thread through some elastic for the waistband, which will take all of fifteen minutes, but I always finish mine with some ribbon or cotton tape around the hemline. This is a cheap, cheerful way of dressing girls beautifully.

you will need:

● Fabric (the length depends on the child – see step 1)

● 0.5m of 1cm-wide elastic

● 1.5m ribbon

method

1 First, cut your fabric. Use the full width of a piece of fabric and cut the length accordingly. Measure from the waist to wherever you want the skirt to fall to and add 4cm.

2 Sew the selvedges together with the right side of the fabric facing in, leaving a 1cm seam allowance. Because you are sewing the selvedges together, there's no need to worry about the edges fraying. (This is why I use a full width of fabric whenever I can when making.)

3 Make the waistband. Fold over 1cm of fabric towards the wrong side of the fabric, then fold over again by 2cm to make a 2cm hem. Sew almost all the way around. Leave a gap of 1.5cm open for threading the elastic through the channel you've created.

4 Now sew the hem. The beauty of using ribbon here is that it adds a gorgeous finishing touch and makes for a very quick and easy way of giving the skirt a professional, neat finish. Fold over 1cm of fabric outwards towards the right side of the fabric (i.e., in the opposite direction to the way in which you would normally fold a hem). The raw edge of the fabric will be on the right side of the skirt. Position the ribbon over this folded hem so that the raw edge is hidden under it. Pin the ribbon onto the skirt all the way around. Overlap the ribbon where the ends meet and fold the top end under so that it doesn't fray. Sew the ribbon onto the skirt twice – once along the top of the ribbon and once along the bottom.

5 The easiest way in which to thread elastic through a waistband is to use a bodkin. If you don't have one, use a safety pin to draw it through the channel. Once the elastic is threaded through, knot it loosely. You can tie the waistband to size when the skirt is on your child.

cosy baggies

Baggies look so cute on kids – not just as pyjamas, but as comfortable, casual daywear, too. They look gorgeous, but cost very little to make.

method

1 Fold a pair of trousers in half at the waist, with 1 leg on top of the other, and flatten them out. This will give you your basic template. Fold the 2 pieces of fabric in half lengthways, with the right sides facing in, and put 1 on top of the other with the folded edges aligned. Place the trousers on top, with the outsides of the legs aligned against the folded sides of the fabric, and pin the whole lot together to keep it all in place.

2 Cutting through the 4 layers of fabric, cut out a rectangle around the folded trousers. Ensure you leave 3cm above the waistband of the original trousers, and 3cm below the bottom of them. Add 4cm to the pointed part of the crotch, to give you the width of the rectangle (see diagram).

3 Now create the crotch. Starting 2.5cm in from the top right of the rectangle, cut off a curve that tapers down to the right-hand edge of the rectangle to a point that is parallel to the pointed part of the crotch on the original trousers (see diagram).

4 Unfold the pieces of fabric, place 1 on top of the other with the right sides facing in and align. Each of the cut-off corners is a crotch seam – 1 for the front and 1 for the back. Sew the 2 crotch seams together at each side of the rectangles of fabric with a 1cm seam allowance.

5 Fold so that the crotch seams are centred, and each leg has a fold on the outside. Sew together the 2 inner leg seams with a 1cm seam allowance.

6 Make the waistband by folding the top over twice by 1.5cm each time, so that the frayed edges are tucked inside, and sew around, leaving a 2cm opening. Use a safety pin to thread the elastic through this.

7 The trousers can be hemmed in the normal way – fold over the fabric twice by 1.5cm and sew around. Or you can add a flash of contrasting colour with ribbon or cotton tape. Fold the hem outwards (i.e., in the opposite way to how you would normally fold a hem). Just fold it once, by 1cm more than the width of your ribbon. Pin the ribbon all the way around, covering the raw edge of the hem. Overlap the ribbon where it meets, and fold over the top edge so that it doesn't fray. Sew around twice – once at the top of the ribbon, and once at the bottom. Repeat on the other leg.

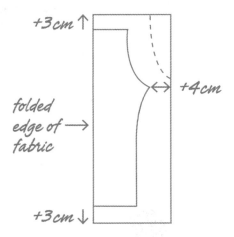

+3cm ↑

+4cm

folded edge of fabric →

+3cm ↓

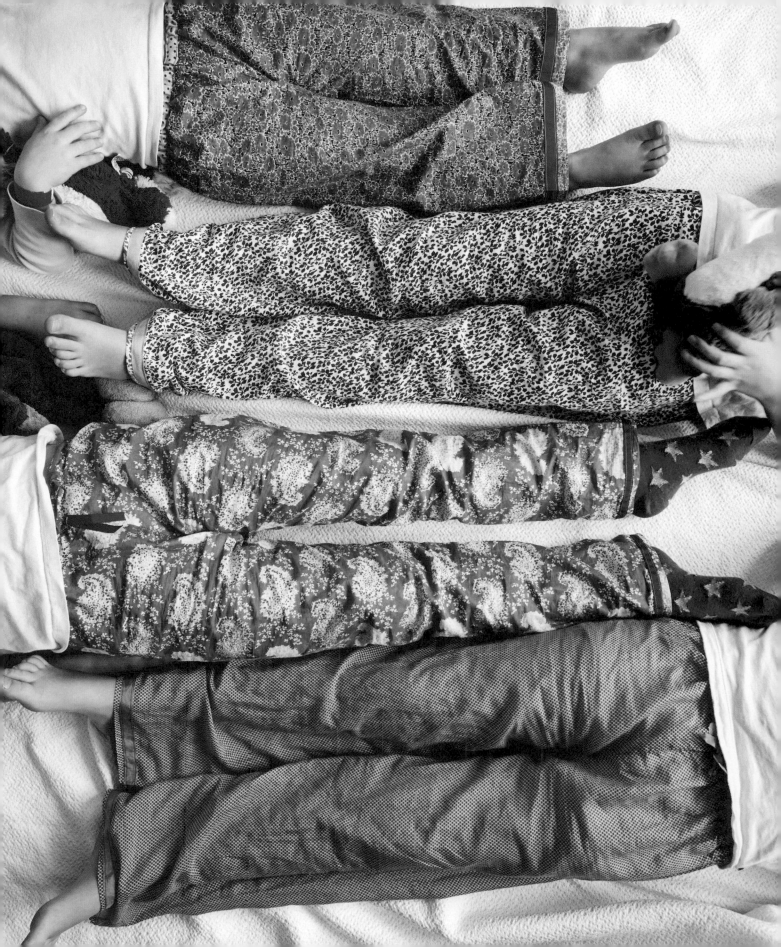

customised plimsolls

A little bit of customisation to a shop-bought basic is always a pleasingly simple way of creating homemade individual style. Plimsoll tongues are just as easy as anything else to whizz through the sewing machine, so this can be done in a flash.

you will need:

- Pair of fabric plimsolls
- Scraps of fabric large enough to cover the tongues of the shoe
- Fabric glue
- 2cm-wide strips of fabric or ribbon

method

1 Remove the laces from the shoes. Pull out the tongues so that they are stretched out. Cut out 2 pieces of fabric that are large enough to cover a tongue. You can cover the inside or outside of the tongue, or both, so if you choose to cover both sides, you'll need 4 pieces of fabric. Don't worry about cutting the exact shape of the tongue from your fabric – just ensure the pieces are bigger, rather than smaller, than the area you want to cover.

2 Spread glue over 1 side of 1 tongue. Press on the fabric. Now repeat on the other side of the tongue, if you've chosen to cover both sides. Repeat with the other tongue. (The glue will hold the fabric in place so you can sew it on easily.)

3 Cut away any excess fabric from around the edges of the tongues. Now pull a tongue as far out of the shoe as you can and machine-stitch around the edge, about 5mm in from the edge. Don't worry about going the whole way around – just sew as far as you can. Repeat with the other shoe.

4 Thread the torn strips of fabric or ribbons through the eyes to use as laces.

tip *When cutting fabric strips or ribbon for the laces, match them to the length of the laces that came with the plimsolls, or double the length for laces that can be criss-crossed up the legs, ballet-shoe style.*

memory book

Of all the things that you can make for your child for Christmas, this one takes more effort, costs a lot less and will be remembered the longest. A memory book is a collection of meaningful stuff that gets accrued over a year. You can fill it with photographs, quotes, mementoes, tickets, school reports, private letters, drawings, cards. I would love to encourage every new parent to make one of these books every year. Yes, it does take some effort, but the reward is so much greater. Imagine if you had a collection of memory books given to you for the first sixteen (or more?) years of your life…

What should you use to fill the memory book? Keep an eye out for: the first time your child writes their name, their first proper drawing, the sweet notes they write to you, a funny letter from their best friend… anything and everything that paints a picture of their life. You could also do a little interview with them to transcribe into the book, covering the usual stuff (what they want to be when they grow up/what is their favourite way to spend time/what they do and don't like and so on).

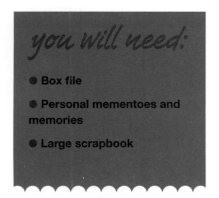

you will need:

● **Box file**

● **Personal mementoes and memories**

● **Large scrapbook**

method

1 To make one of these, you need to become a bit of a hoarder. Every time you see something that might be good for the book, stash it in a dedicated box file. Better to have too much stuff that can be dumped later than to realise you forgot to keep something you wish you had.

2 If you are quite organised, you can make these books as you go through the year. That's the sensible way to do it – in small steps. I never quite manage that and end up doing a big blitz at the end of the year. Either way, as long as you gather stuff as you go, everything will be collated, ready to stick in the book.

3 When you are ready, stick the mementos into the scrapbook in chronological order using stick glue, and write in any quotes and details you would like to add. It's nice to put your voice into it, too, adding commentary on what has been happening during the year, what your child likes and doesn't like, or anything else that makes it personal to your child. You could organise it by month, or by theme – whatever suits you and the lucky recipient.

4 Give this gift separately from the rest of the Christmas presents, so that everyone can sit together and enjoy the memories of the year.

advent calendar

As we all know, the most excitement is sometimes derived from the anticipation of something. My kids love the ritual of the countdown to Christmas so much that they start an informal countdown to the countdown weeks before the 1st of December, updating me each day on how many days there are to go until the advent calendar goes up! You can create a stylish advent calendar very simply using paper envelopes strung along a line.

you will need:

- 2 screw hooks
- String or wire
- 24 envelopes
- 24 wooden pegs
- Glue
- Glitter
- Pen or numbered rubber stamps

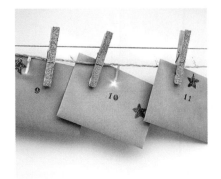

method

1 First, fix up a line for hanging the envelopes. Use a bradawl to make holes in the walls in the positions into which you would like to fix the screw hooks. Screw the hooks into the wall, then tightly knot the ends of the string or wire onto them, pulling it taut to ensure the line doesn't sag. You can leave the line up all year round (I do), to hang bits from for other celebrations, but if you want to take the string down after Christmas, leave the hooks in the wall to make rehanging super easy next year.

2 Number the envelopes from 1 to 24 using a pen or rubber stamps.

3 Spread glue on one side of each peg and cover it in glitter to make them look suitably festive.

4 Filling the advent calendar can be an expensive business, but children love interesting facts, jokes, world records and funny little poems. Hang up envelopes containing these, interspersed with others enclosing chocolate coins, sweets, candy canes, lollipops – any goodies your children like. They can take it in turns to open each envelope. If you've got any children that are too small to read, arrange it so that they open only the sweetie envelopes. If all the children are too young to read, how about putting in a page of a story each day to read to them?

tip *If you don't have rubber stamps with which to stamp numbers onto the envelopes, you could make your own following the instructions on page 138. If you have number stencils, you could use the marker pens through those.*

sackcloth santa sacks

*This project is a simple but stylish take on traditional stockings.
I love the contrast of gold or silver against the rough hessian –
such a great combination.*

you will need:

- Rectangle of hessian measuring 130 x 45cm

- 2 x 60cm lengths of red pompom trim

- 2 x 120cm lengths of ribbon or thick string

- Bodkin or safety pin

- 40 x 60cm rectangle of sticky backed plastic

- Fine-tipped permanent marker

- Craft knife

method

1 First, make the sack. Fold the hessian in half widthways. Run a length of pompom trim down each side, with the pompoms inside the fabric and the edging sandwiched in between the hessian edges. The trim is 5cm shorter than the sides, which will leave 5cm at the top of each side untrimmed. Pin the hessian and trim together on each side.

2 Machine-stitch the sides of the sack together, ensuring you sew through the pompom edging (go by eye and feel).

3 Fold the top of the sack over twice to make a deep hem and a channel for the drawstring. Pin this in place, then sew around the top of the sack to secure the hem.

4 Turn the sack the right way out so that the seams are inside and the pompoms are on the outside.

5 Thread the first length of ribbon or string through the top hem. You'll need to start and finish it at 1 side of the sack; the other will be threaded through from the opposite side, so that you pull the strings away from each other to pull the sack shut. Using a bodkin is the easiest way to do this. First, use a pencil to make 2 holes in the hem, 1 on either side of a side seam. Push the point of the pencil through the fabric to part the threads, then wiggle it around a little to enlarge the hole. Now use the bodkin to thread the drawstring. (If you don't have a bodkin, pin the drawstring onto a safety pin and use that to pull the string through the channel. You'll need to pull apart the weave a bit more to make a gap big enough to fit the safety pin through.) Knot the ends of each drawstring.

6 Using the permanent marker, draw a design on the shiny side of the sticky backed plastic. Cut it out with the craft knife to make a stencil.

7 Peel off the backing from the sticky backed plastic and stick the stencil onto the sack. Put some newspaper or a bin bag inside the sack (to prevent paint seeping through to the other side of the bag) and use spray paint to paint the design. Leave to dry, then peel off the plastic.

Epiphany crowns

The Epiphany, on 6th January, marks the occasion of the visit of the Three Wise Men to Jesus, Mary and Joseph. In many Christian countries it passes unobserved, save for the fact that it is the date by which all Christmas decorations must be taken down. But in Spain it is an important holiday, when presents are given to remember the gifts from the three kings to the baby Jesus. In some South American countries, it is the Wise Men who bring Christmas gifts, not Father Christmas. And in France, special cakes (galettes des Rois) are everywhere, parties are thrown and children wear crowns. So here's how to make some beautiful crowns, not just for Epiphany, but for any day on which a child wants to be a prince or princess.
(Actually, isn't that most days?)

you will need:

- Rectangle of heavyweight fabric measuring 30 x 12cm, preferably with a chunky weave, such as linen or denim

- Gold, silver or white paint

- Glitter and fake jewels (optional)

- Craft glue (optional)

- 20cm piece of 5mm-wide elastic

- 25 x 50cm piece of netting (optional)

method

1 Lay out your rectangle of fabric. Cut a 5cm-deep zig zag along the top edge of the crown (one of the long sides of the fabric).

2 Lay the fabric on a sheet of newspaper. Load up a paintbrush very generously with paint and paint a fairly thick coat all over the fabric. You can paint both sides. Or, if you paint one side only and use a different coloured paint to the fabric, you will get a patchy effect on the underside where paint has seeped through, which looks really cool. Hang the fabric on a line to dry.

3 Once it's dry, wrap the fabric around to make a crown shape. Machine- or hand-stitch the ends together. Stick on the glitter and jewels, if you are using them, with craft glue.

4 Stitch each end of the elastic onto the crown so that it goes around the back of the head.

5 If you want to add a train, gather together the short end of the netting and stitch the gathered end of the fabric onto the elastic at the back of the crown.

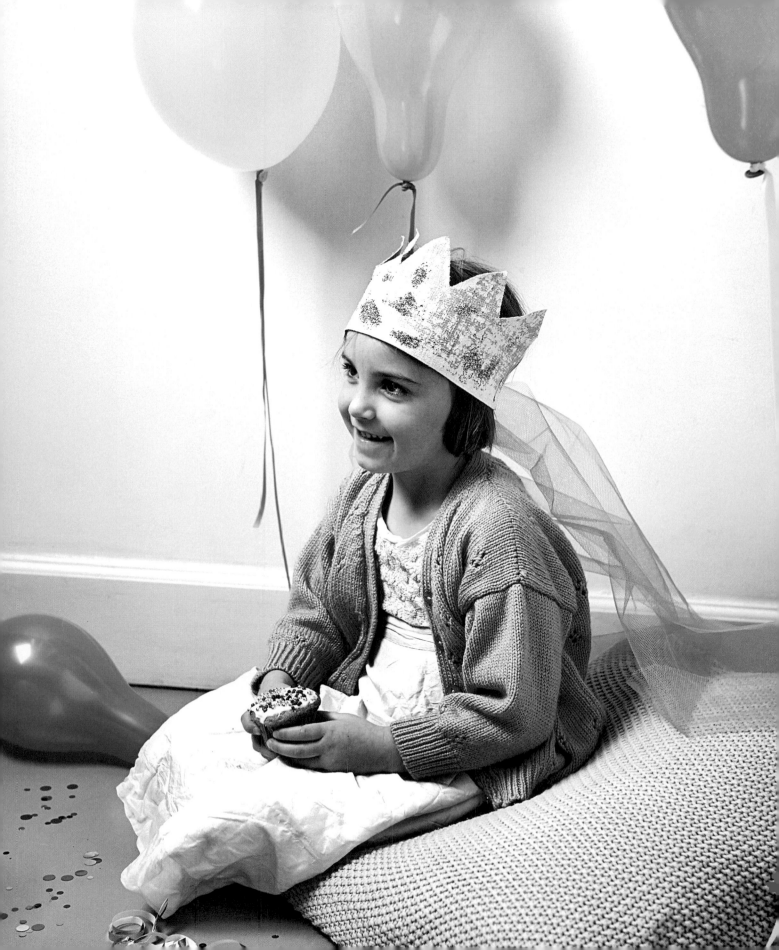

feather cake ribbon

This looks so beautiful wrapped around a celebration cake and is one of those things that can be pulled out year after year, imbued with tradition and memories. As it requires quite a lot of feathers, it gives a good incentive to get out and about with the children to find your own, or you can buy white and coloured quill feathers cheaply from craft stores.

you will need:

- **30–40 feathers**
- **Coloured spray paint or paint**
- **2 x 1m-long strips of 6cm-wide fabric**
- **Craft glue**

method

1 If you need to colour your feathers, put them on some foil or baking paper and spray with spray paint or paint with a brush. Using foil or baking paper means that the paint sticks and the feathers should peel away when dry.

2 Spread glue along 1 of the strips of fabric. Lay out the feathers along the glue so that the shafts are stuck down and the feathers extend beyond the fabric strip. Put extra glue on top of the shafts, then align the second fabric strip over the first so that the shafts are sandwiched between them.

3 Machine-stitch the strips together, with 2 rows of stitches – 1 row 5mm from the top and the other row 5mm from the bottom.

4 Wrap the cake ribbon around the sides of your cake and fix with a couple of pins, sticking them through the ribbon and into the cake. Pinning it means you can easily undo it to cut the cake and makes it easy to reuse the cake-ribbon year after year.

note *Wrap the ribbon up in tissue paper and store it in an old shoebox to protect the feathers, so it looks just as good every time you pull it out.*

feathered headdress

The feather cake-ribbon project (page 159) can be scaled down into this feathered headdress (pictured on page 162). It makes the best birthday crown for any boy or girl to wear to their party, and is great for fancy dress, too.

you will need:

- 20 feathers
- Various coloured paints
- 30cm-long strip of double-sided tape
- 2 x 30cm lengths of 6cm-wide colourful fabric
- 20cm length of 2cm-wide elastic

method

1 Paint the feathers in an array of colours. Leave some unpainted, too.

2 Stick the double-sided tape along the middle of 1 of the strips of fabric on the wrong side. Fix the shafts of the feathers to the tape, allowing the feathers themselves to extend beyond the fabric. Align the second piece of fabric on top with the right side facing out.

3 Machine-stitch a row of stitches along the top and the bottom of the fabric-feather sandwich. Be careful not to sew through the double-sided tape because it will make your needle sticky and will stop the machine from working properly.

4 Sew the ends of the elastic into the fabric band to complete the crown.

cake bunting

It's lovely to put a message on a cake, or pile of little cakes, with this pretty cake bunting. It saves you having to pipe letters out of icing, which is not easy. Plus, this looks really cute!

you will need:

● **Length of string or thread a little longer than the span of the cake(s)**

● **Washi tape**

● **Fine-tipped permanent marker pen or rubber stamps (you can make your own stamps following the instructions on page 138)**

● **2 cocktail sticks or bamboo skewers**

method

1 To make each flag, fold a small rectangle of Washi tape over a length of string and press the sticky sides together. You'll need 1 flag per letter, so work out how many you will need and space them out across the string accordingly.

2 Write or stamp out your message on the flags.

3 Fix the string onto the cocktail sticks by knotting 1 end of the string tightly around each stick. Now press the cocktail sticks into the cake(s). (Don't put the bunting right next to the candles, for obvious reasons.)

note *This bunting can also be used to spell out a birthday message on a front door. Just use extra tape to stick it up.*

fairy light birthday bunting

This isn't really bunting, in that it requires no real making or sewing – it's simply an easy assembly job. It looks so, so pretty, though, just hung along a wall or suspended over a party table.

you will need:

- Long string of fairy lights
- Strips of ribbon and torn fabric

method

Simply tie the strips of ribbon and fabric onto the light string. That's it. Suspend the string of lights over the party table, then switch it on. So cute!

note *If you have any clip-on birds, butterflies or anything else, they look gorgeous suspended from the string of lights, too. And don't hide this away between birthdays – hang it up in a bedroom instead.*

tip *Try this with your Christmas tree lights. Tie on bows of red, silver and gold ribbon for festive magic.*

balloon piñatas

Balloon piñatas are a cheap and easy take on hanging piñatas. I love papier-mâché piñatas because they look so pretty, but what always puts me off is the fact that they're almost impossible for children to break their way into. The game of trying to crack one open can go on for ages and ages until a parent takes control of the bat and kills it in a slightly disturbing, aggressive fashion. So here's a great little-kid friendly option... well, actually, an any-kid friendly option.

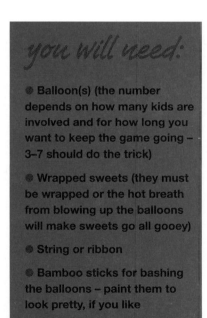

you will need:

● Balloon(s) (the number depends on how many kids are involved and for how long you want to keep the game going – 3–7 should do the trick)

● Wrapped sweets (they must be wrapped or the hot breath from blowing up the balloons will make sweets go all gooey)

● String or ribbon

● Bamboo sticks for bashing the balloons – paint them to look pretty, if you like

method

1 First, stretch out a balloon by blowing it up. Let it deflate, then stretch out the neck of the balloon as much as you can. Get someone else to pour in as many sweets as will fit while you hold open the neck. Stretch the rubber a little more by blowing up the balloon again and allowing it to deflate. Now stuff in as many more sweets as you can. Blow up the balloon and knot it. Repeat the process until all your balloons are filled.

2 Tie on string or ribbon to each balloon so that it is ready for hanging.

3 Put up a line to suspend your row of balloons from. If you have hooks in the wall from hanging an advent calendar (see page 151), these could be ideal for this job. If you have a tree to hang the balloons from, suspend them from different branches. Using bamboo sticks, the children can take it in turns to whack the balloons, or several can have a go at once.

magic floating napkin

Children absolutely love magic tricks and, happily, seem to get just as much enjoyment from a dad or uncle performing them as a professional. Maybe more so, actually, because then they can bask in the adulation of their friends, who think their dad has special powers. You can keep the kids entertained with tricks you can buy online or from a joke shop, such as a disappearing handkerchief or coins, or light-up thumbs. However, this trick, introduced to my kids by their uncle, is my all-time favourite and it requires no special kit or skill. The children can do it, too. For some reason, no matter how often I see it – and even though I know how it is done – it still entrances me, because it just looks so freaky.

you will need:

● **Napkin or other piece of fabric (it must be totally opaque)**

● **Knife (the sort you eat with, not a sharp one)**

method

1 To perform the trick, put the knife under 1 of the corners of the napkin and pick up the knife and fabric together, holding them in your right hand (or left, if you are left-handed). Hold the adjacent corner of the napkin in your other hand. The knife must be hidden from view by the fabric.

2 Waft your hands back and forth as if you are waving them gently. The knife will lift up the fabric in a way that looks as if a supernatural force is pulling it from the other side.

final thought

Making stuff with children has obvious appeal in the 'how to fill time' sense, but beyond the immediate placating of a bored child, there's a bigger prize. Encouraging creativity through letting a child see how one thing can very easily be turned into another helps them learn how to occupy themselves. Everyone knows if you give a child a pot of pens and a piece of plain paper, their imagination will take over. But it's a natural ability that can be lost if it's not cherished. We know how, as adults, a blank sheet intimidates rather than excites us. Children just see things differently. A pile of safety pins. Wooden blocks. Fabric. Feathers and glue. They'll turn it all into something. And if that ability to see things differently – creativity – carries through into adulthood, who knows where it might lead.

'Creativity is just connecting things. When you ask creative people how they did something, they feel a little guilty because they didn't really do it, they just saw something. It seemed obvious to them after a while.'
– Steve Jobs

I'm not saying that family life should be a fest of home making. Clearly we don't all have time for that. And I'm not saying crafting trumps screen time, reading or anything else.

But making isn't just about sitting at a table crafting in a conventional way. It's anything you do yourself. So, next time you're drilling a hole, painting a wall or cooking, let your kids see what you're doing and, if they can, let them join in. It might be mundane to us, but don't forget, kids see things differently.

resources

UK

● CASTORS: www.castors-online.co.uk

● FABRICS:
Liberty of London (www.liberty.co.uk)
The Cloth Shop, Portobello, London W10 (www.theclothshop.net)
Classic Textiles, Goldhawk Road, London W12 (www.classic-textiles.com)
Entree des Fournisseurs, Paris (www.entreedesfournisseurs.fr)

● FELT OFFCUTS: www.ebay.co.uk

● FLUORO PINK FABRIC PAINT: Pebeo Setacolor Fabric Paint (www.pebeo.com)

● FRUIT CRATES: Kempton Park antiques market or www.ebay.co.uk

● GLOW-IN-THE-DARK PAINT: Brian Clegg (www.brianclegg.co.uk – available through many stockists – search online)

● I HEART YOU PICTURE FRAME: Ikea (www.ikea.com)

● KRAFT PAPER ENVELOPES: Paperchase (www.paperchase.co.uk)

● MAGNETS: www.first4magnets.com

● MAGNETIC STEEL CUT TO SIZE: www.metals4u.co.uk

● PRINTERS TRAY: (www.ebay.co.uk)

● RIBBONS:
Lyndons Stitch and Beads, Portobello Road, London W11
V V Rouleaux (www.vvrouleaux.com)

● SPRAY PAINT (ON THE PRINTER'S TRAY TOY): Liquitex from Cass art (www.cassart.co.uk)

● ROWAN COCOON WOOL: www.woolwarehouse.co.uk

● WOODEN WINE BOXES: Majestic Wine Warehouse. Wine shops should let you have empty ones for a small donation.

With thanks to Mamas & Papas, Paperchase, Talking Tables and VV Rouleaux for loaning equipment and props used in this book.

AUSTRALIA

● **BIG W** (www.b gw.com.au)
Fabrics, ribbons, sewing supplies and craft materials.

● **BUNNINGS WAREHOUSE** (www.bunnings.com.au)
Woodwork materials and castors.

● **EBAY** (www.ebay.com.au)

● **IKEA** (www.ikea.com/au/en)

● **SUNSPUN** (www.sunspun.com.au)
Wool and knitting supplies.

NEW ZEALAND

● **BUNNINGS WAREHOUSE** (www.bunnings.com.au)
Woodwork materials and castors.

● **KNIT WORLD** (www.knitworld.co.nz) & **SKEINZ** (www.skeinz.com)
Wool and knitting supplies.

● **SPOTLIGHT** (www.spotlight.co.nz)
Fabrics, ribbons and sewing supplies.

SOUTH AFRICA

● **ART ATTACK** (www.artattack.co.za) & **SA ART SUPPLIES** (www.sasupplies.com)
Arts and crafts supplies.

● **DAWANDA** (www.en.dawanda.com)
Fabrics, ribbons and sewing supplies.

● **EBAY** (www.ebay.co.za)

● **WOOL I KNIT** (www.wooliknit.co.za)
Wool and knitting supplies.

index

thank you!

Thank you to everyone who's worked on this book, for the flair and hard work you always deliver.

Thank you to my friends and family who are always there, supporting, loving and making me laugh, especially when the going gets tough.

Thank you Maya, Iona, Honor, Noah, Theo, Kitty, Beatrice, Lola, Nefertiti, Etta, Rosie and Georgina – my beauties, you rock!

And, thank you for buying this book.

I hope you like it and that it inspires you and yours to enjoy many happy hours of making.

Love Joanna xxx